Writing for Academic Purposes

英作文を卒業して英語論文を書く

田地野 彰
ティム・スチュワート 編
デビッド・ダルスキー

Copyright © Akira Tajino, Tim Stewart, and David Dalsky 2010
First published 2010
Reprinted with corrections 2011

All rights reserved. Except for the quotation of short passages for the purposes of criticism and review, no part of this publication may be reproduced, stored in a retrieval system, or transmitted in any form or by any means, electronic, mechanical, photocopying, recording or otherwise, without the written prior permission of the publisher.
In case of photocopying and electronic copying and retrieval from network personally, permission will be given on receipts of payment and making inquiries. For details please contact us through e-mail. Our e-mail address is given below.

Book Design © Yoshiharu Osaki

Hituzi Syobo Publishing
Yamato bldg. 2F, 2-1-2 Sengoku Bunkyo-ku Tokyo, Japan
112-0011

phone +81-3-5319-4916 fax +81-3-5319-4917
e-mail: toiawase@hituzi.co.jp
http://www.hituzi.co.jp/
postal transfer 00120-8-142852

ISBN978-4-89476-490-3
Printed in Japan

Preface

Academic writing skills are crucial to success at university. Writing is the communication tool that connects international academic communities. In fact, it is not an exaggeration to say that without developing the ability to express yourself in the conventions of academic written discourse you will remain voiceless as a university scholar.

This book is intended to provide those who have little experience in academic writing with opportunities to learn about the nature of academic writing and to practice writing academic texts. For this purpose, the book consists of three main parts.

Part I is devoted to a discussion of the nature of academic writing. Each of the five chapters takes the form of a research paper; i.e., the chapter starts with a title, which is followed by an abstract, a list of key words, an introduction, a main body organized in sections which mark the logical development of the argument, and a conclusion. In addition, most importantly, the sources of concepts and information used in the chapter which were found in the work of other researchers are cited in the text, and complete information about all the sources of information used is listed in a references section. It is expected that the readers of this book will come to understand the typical structure of research papers as they read about the nature of research papers. Thus, Part I describes the target: writing academic research papers.

Part II focuses attention on how to reach the target step-by-step. Supportive learning tasks that recognize the gap between students' current writing skills and the target will provide useful opportunities to practice. In other words, Part I takes a Learn-by-Thinking approach from a teacher's perspective and Part II, from a student's perspective, a Learn-by-Doing approach.

In addition, in Part III, three lessons from English-for-General-Academic-Purposes (EGAP) academic writing courses at Kyoto University are included to welcome readers to feel involved in our EGAP courses at Kyoto University.

It is our sincere hope that this book will be of some help to university students in Japan, and also, of some use for teachers of academic writing courses. The Chinese philosopher, Confucius, stated: "Tell me, and I will forget. Show me, and I may remember. Involve me, and I will understand." We will be satisfied if this book inspires our readers to get involved in their own development as scholars and researchers.

Suggestions for Using the Book

This book may be more useful than a conventional course textbook because it can serve as a reference book for teachers and learners, as well as a resource book for writers. In addition, this book can be used as a main course book or as a supplementary text in academic reading and vocabulary building courses, as well as in courses for academic writing. It is meant to help writers whose first language is not English, but native writers of academic English may also learn something from this book about the nature of academic writing.

The book is designed so that teachers and learners can make their own decisions about how they will use it. We expect that teachers and students will be able to use this book to strengthen their own unique teaching and learning styles. We trust that experienced teachers, for instance, will find ways to use this book to deal with the special academic writing needs of their own groups of learners. We would be disappointed if teachers simply let the book make all the decisions about what to teach and how to best help their students.

That said, we would like to share our own ten-point guideline for the way we are using this book with our own classes. The following suggestions were written from a teacher's perspective. If you are a learner using this book independently, remember that you are your own teacher.

1. Go beyond writing-skill building. Teach to assumptions, expectations and attitudes about academic writing.

2. Pay special attention to research papers, among the various types of academic writing.

3. Give the students experiences reading a wide variety of models of what they will be expected to write. Give examples of analytical readings of texts.

4. Begin with Part I. Spend the first weeks of the course thinking about the nature of academic writing and studying examples of published texts before students begin writing.

5. Put a special on-going emphasis on helping students learn new words which are important for their academic fields. Provide them with academic word lists.

6. Place vocabulary learning in context. Enrich contextual vocabulary learning by showing students how to get information about collocations and by giving them examples of discourse analysis applied to research papers.

7. Encourage "team learning." Support students in learning how to form and sustain effective reading and writing teams.

8. Challenge the students, as a team, to write the components of a short research paper (e.g., title, abstract, or research questions) which is based on a research project that the students can actually carry out themselves.

9. Apply critical thinking to the process of writing revisions.

10. Link academic reading and writing in Japanese with learning to write in English.

To sum up, this book offers both teachers and learners a wide variety of opportunities for academic skill development—use it creatively.

Contents

Preface 1
Suggestions for Using the Book 3

Part I
Key Issues in Academic Writing
Introduction to Part I (Japanese)

Chapter 1	The Primary Features of Academic Writing 9
Chapter 2	Understanding the Structure of Research Papers 19
Chapter 3	Academic Vocabulary and Academic Writing 31
Chapter 4	Critical Thinking and Reading Research Papers 47
Chapter 5	Critical Reading: An Application of Critical Thinking 57

Part II
Writing an Academic Paper
Introduction to Part II (Japanese)

Chapter 6	Writing the Outline and the First Draft 73
Chapter 7	Researching an Academic Paper 89
Chapter 8	Writing the Abstract 113
Chapter 9	Writing the Introduction 123
Chapter 10	Writing the Body Section 135
Chapter 11	Writing the Conclusion 151
Chapter 12	Citing Sources and Writing the References Section 161

Part III
Academic Writing Classes at Kyoto University
Introduction to Part III (Japanese)

Chapter 13	Focusing on Structure: Comparison and Contrast 177
Chapter 14	Peer Review: Editing an Academic Paper 187
Chapter 15	Academic Writing in the Hybrid Classroom 201

Index 209
Notes on the Contributors 212

Part I

Key Issues in Academic Writing

Introduction to
Part I

　アカデミックライティングの世界へようこそ．パートIでは，アカデミックライティングの基本的な考え方を学ぶ．これまで学習してきたであろう「英作文」とこれから学ぶ「アカデミックライティング」は，同じ「書く」という行為でありながら，その内実はずいぶんと異なる．まずは，しっかりとアカデミックライティングの概念を学ぶことによって，表層的ではない本質的な考え方を身につけてほしい．専門分野に左右されない本質を学ぶことによって，あなたが今後，どのような専門分野に進もうとも，アカデミックライティングに関して迷うことはないだろう．アカデミックライティングを始めとする学術分野での英語は，一般目的の英語とはどのような点で異なるのか，また「なぜ」異なっているのかを考えながら読み進めてほしい．

　パートIは5章からなり，それぞれが一つの論文の体裁を取っている．したがって，読み進めるうちに論文のスタイルというものに自然に慣れることができるだろう．各章の最初と最後には日本語の解説が加えられているので，まずはそちらに目を通し，全体を想像しながら読み進めていってほしい．1章では，アカデミックライティングの特徴について説明する．2章では，英語学術論文の構造について見ていく．3章では，アカデミックライティングに用いられる語彙について紹介する．4章と5章では，アカデミックライティングに必要となる学術論文の読み方と考え方について学ぶことになる．

Chapter I

The Primary Features of Academic Writing

Abstract

This chapter discusses some issues which are central to understanding the nature of academic writing. Indeed, a specific definition of academic writing for university students in Japan has not yet been agreed upon and this chapter proposes a set of defining criteria and outlines the primary features of academic writing. By discussing the features common to research papers in all disciplines, the chapter aims to support students in the development of competence in one genre of academic writing, the research paper. The chapter also describes the scope of the academic area we are interested in: English for General Academic Purposes (EGAP).

Keywords

Academic community, Academic writing, EAP, EGAP, ESAP, Genre

この章のねらい

この章では学術論文を中心としたアカデミックライティングの考え方について紹介する．そもそもアカデミックライティングとは何か，また，どのような性質を持っているものなのだろうか．一番の特徴は，読者の範囲が限定されているというものである．そのため，いくつかのルールが暗に明に定められている．これから学習するアカデミックライティングは，これまで学習してきた英作文と比べてどのような点で異なるのかに注意して読み進めていってほしい．後半では，アカデミックライティングを含めた，より広い概念である「学術目的の英語 English for Academic Purposes（EAP）」の考え方についても紹介する．

1. Introduction

It is reasonable to claim that writing is crucial to academic success in higher education since students' assessments, in many cases, are primarily based on their written work in various genres of academic writing ranging from course reports to research dissertations. It is important for you to recognize that academic success depends not only on the content of your written work but also on the way you write your reports and dissertations[1]. In fact, it is not an exaggeration to say that without developing the ability to express yourself in the conventions of academic written discourse you will remain voiceless at university. However, academic writing in English, despite recognition of its importance, often presents daunting challenges for many university English-as-a-Foreign-Language (EFL) students (see Jordan, 1997). Indeed, anecdotal evidence suggests that this is especially true for undergraduate students at all English proficiency levels. Yet, what is it that makes academic writing so difficult for Japanese university students? In order to answer this question, it is necessary to clarify the nature of academic writing. This is the main purpose of the present chapter.

2. Academic writing: Defining criteria and key characteristics

Academic writing addresses "general" (interdisciplinary) as well as "specific" (within a discipline) audiences. There are also various genres of academic writing; e.g., essays, course term reports, examination answers, book reviews, research papers, and graduate school dissertations. Swales (1990, p. 58) provides a clear definition of genre by stating, "A genre comprises a class of communicative events, the members of which share some set [sic - *some set* means *a set*] of communicative purposes." In this book, our genre (i.e., the class of communicative events) of interest is the research paper; the shared public purpose is to present a written report of new research; and the participants are members of the academic community of all people interested in the findings of that particular research.

Each genre has its own unique "content structure or format, style, and various conventions" (Jordan, 1997, p. 166). While accepting the differences among these genres, however, they share certain essential features. Ann Johns (1997) in her book *Text, Role, and Context: Developing Academic Literacies* has drawn up a useful list of ten fundamental features of academic writing based on the views of two leading composition theorists, Elbow (1991) and Purves (1990), as well as on the research of Geertz (1988), an anthropologist who has studied the writings of academic communities. According to Johns (1997, pp. 58–63), all academic written texts share the following characteristics:

1) Texts must be explicit.
2) Topic and argument should be prerevealed in the introduction.
3) Writers should provide "maps" or "signposts" for the readers throughout the texts, telling the readers where they have been in the text and where they are going.
4) The language of texts should create a distance between the writer and the text to give the appearance of objectivity.
5) Texts should maintain a "rubber-gloved" [i.e., an unemotional or detached] *quality of voice and register.*
6) Writers should take a guarded stance [i.e., a cautious position], *especially when presenting argumentation and results.*
7) Texts should display a vision of reality shared by members of the particular discourse community to which the text is addressed (or to the particular faculty member who made the assignment).
8) Academic texts should display a set of social and authority relations; they should show the writer's understanding of the roles they play within the text or context [i.e., the writing style should be appropriate for an academic setting].
9) Academic texts should acknowledge the complex and important nature of intertextuality, the exploitation of other texts without resorting to plagiarism.
10) Texts should comply with the genre requirements of the community or classroom.
(Note that the comments enclosed in square parentheses were added by the authors of this book.)

Thus, the features of academic texts include the use of:

1) academic vocabulary, whenever necessary, to present all messages of the paper absolutely clearly (e.g., dependent and independent variables,

statistically significant differences, socio-economic constraints);
2) organizational structure of the text at micro- and macro- levels (e.g., at the micro-level, an inductive top-down pattern with topic sentences followed by supporting arguments or evidence at the paragraph level, and at the macro-level, an "introduction-method-results-conclusion" flow throughout the entire paper);
3) metadiscourse features (e.g., the use of words such as *"argue," "show," "firstly,"* and *"in conclusion"*);
4) expressions to indicate neutrality and objectivity (e.g., the tendency to avoid using the first-person singular pronoun to represent the writer: *"I," "my," "me," "mine,"* and expressions such as *"I feel"* or *"I think"*);
5) hedges (e.g., the use of modals like *"may"* and *"might"* and other expressions such as *"it seems"* and *"it is possible that"* to cautiously report your own findings);
6) acknowledgments of previous studies and research reports to avoid plagiarism (e.g., the inclusion of a literature review, the use of in-text citations, and the listing of sources of information in a references section); and
7) compliance with the genre requirements of a specific academic community (e.g., research papers in social psychology use commonly-accepted types of statistical analyses to objectively test hypotheses).

Moreover, academic writing can be characterized as "a product of such considerations as *audience, purpose, organization, style, flow,* and *presentation*" (Swales & Feak, 1994, p.7). We have added to sensible suggestions made by Holst (1995) in recommending that the following questions may form a useful guideline for academic writers:

1) What is your purpose in writing?
2) Who are you writing for?
3) What should your text look like (i.e., the conventional organization of the particular type of writing)?
4) What language features and tone should you adopt to realize your purpose?

3. EGAP and academic writing at university

Research from the literature of English for Academic Purposes (EAP) will help us identify the scope of the academic writing area we are interested in, English for General Academic Purposes (EGAP), rather than English for Specific Academic Purposes (ESAP). We hope that this EGAP writing book will be of use to undergraduate students of any academic discipline who have had little experience in learning how to write research papers. It is important to note that we are not arguing that writing is the same in all disciplines, but rather we are focusing more on common features than on differences. The EGAP perspective is clarified in Figure 1.1.

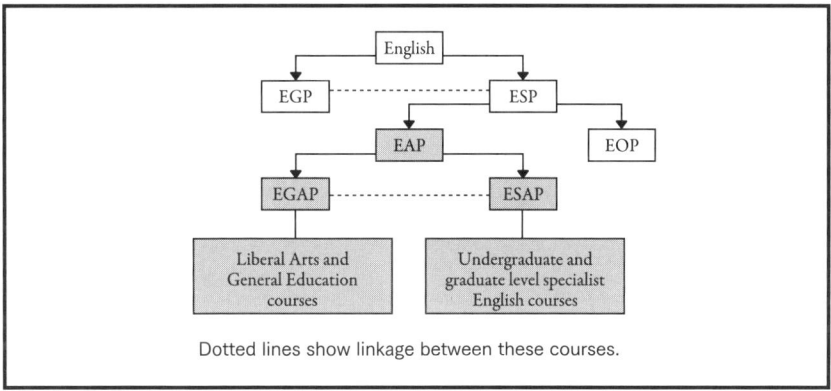

Figure 1.1 Objectives of university English education (Tajino & Suiko, 2005)

The diagram shown in Figure 1.1 was made by borrowing a framework from EAP literature (e.g., Blue, 1988; Dudley-Evans & St John, 1998; Jordan, 1997). As you can see in the diagram, English can be divided into the two categories: EGP (English for General Purposes) and ESP (English for Specific Purposes). EGP deals with English language skills for general purposes (e.g., for the purpose of talking about the weather in casual conversation), while ESP is concerned with the development of language skills for a particular purpose (e.g., passing English proficiency examinations). Furthermore, ESP can be classified into EAP and EOP (English for Occupational Purposes). EAP education may take place in academic contexts (e.g., learning how to read and write research papers) and EOP education may also take place in university settings but it is more closely related to successful job performance (e.g., communicative English skills necessary for doctors to function successfully at work).

In addition, EAP can be categorized into EGAP and ESAP. EGAP refers to language skills which may be required in any discipline, whereas ESAP refers to language skills which may be required in only one particular discipline. At Kyoto University, for example, *Zengaku Kyotsu Kamoku Eigo,* the Liberal Arts and General Education English courses offered by the Faculty of Integrated Human Studies aim to deal with EGAP; while *Senmon Eigo,* the discipline-specific English courses offered by other faculties fall into the category of ESAP. It is important to note that EGAP and ESAP courses are expected to link to each other in the curriculum. The relationship between these two sets of courses is clarified in Figure 1.2 below.

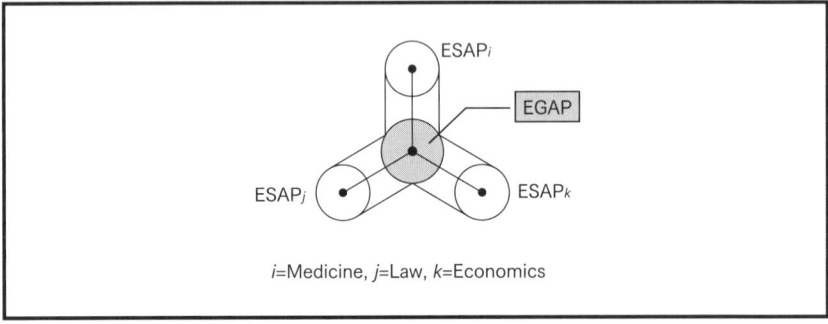

Figure 1.2 Relationship between EGAP and ESAP (Tajino, 2004)

In the diagram the area in the center, which every discipline shares in common, refers to EGAP; i.e., the scope of this book.

4. Conclusion

University students in Japan who are interested in research foresee roles for themselves in international academic communities. You can add credibility to your membership in such communities by developing communicative English language skills which will allow you to be an active participant in realizing the common goals of your academic community. In the following chapters, we hope that we will inspire you to read and write in English. We will provide you with insights into the nature of academic writing and also with practical advice to help you develop your own skills as a writer. In addition, we will introduce a genre approach to the analysis of academic writing, discuss the role of academic vocabulary in research papers, and consider the vital role of critical thinking in the reading and writing of research papers.

References

Blue, G. (1988). Individualising academic writing tuition. In P. C. Robinson (Ed.), *Academic writing: Process and product*. ELT Documents 129.

Dudley-Evans, T., & St John, M. J. (1998). *Developments in English for specific purposes*. Cambridge: Cambridge University Press.

Elbow, P. (1991). Reflections on academic discourse: How it relates to freshmen and colleagues. *College English, 53*(2), 135–155.

Geertz, C. (1988). *Works and lives: The anthropologist as author*. Stanford: Stanford University Press.

Holst, J. (1995). *Writ 101: Writing English*. Wellington: Victoria University Press.

Johns, A. (1997). *Text, role and context: Developing academic literacies*. Cambridge: Cambridge University Press.

Jordan, R. R. (1997). *English for academic purposes: A guide and resource book for teachers*. Cambridge: Cambridge University Press.

Purves, A. C. (1990). *The scribal society: An essay on literacy and schooling in the information age*. New York: Longman.

Swales, J. M. (1990). *Genre analysis: English in academic and research settings*. Cambridge: Cambridge University Press.

Swales, J. M., & Feak, C. B. (1994). *Academic writing for graduate students: A course for nonnative speakers of English*. Ann Arbor: University of Michigan Press.

Tajino, A. (2004). Nihon ni okeru daigaku eigokyoiku no mokuteki to mokuhyo ni tsuite–ESP kenkyu karano shisa [On the aims and objectives of university English language education in Japan: An ESP perspective], *MM News, 7*, 11–21.

Tajino, A., & Suiko, M. (2005). Daigaku eigokyoiku eno teigen–Karikyuramu kaihatsu eno shisutemu apurochi [A proposal for university English language education: A systems approach to curriculum development]. In Y. Takefuta, & M. Suiko (Eds.), *Korekarano Daigaku Eigokyoiku* [The Future of University English Language Education] (pp. 1–46). Tokyo: Iwanami Shoten.

Note

1. In this book, the second-person singular pronoun *"you"* is deliberately used for a pedagogical purpose; *"you"* refers to a reader of the textbook, a student, and *"we"* refers to the authors.

Learning Tasks

1) Go to the university library, or visit the library's on-line journal search section, and select a research paper from an academic journal in your own research field. Examine the paper to discover what sections the paper contains. Read the section in which previous studies are discussed. Find out how the research questions and methodology are described. Study the ways the findings of the research are shown in figures, or otherwise explained.

2) There is a section in academic journals called "Notes to Contributors" or "Instructions to Authors." This information is a set of guidelines for people who wish to submit research papers to be considered for publication. The information includes details about the length of the paper, the writing style requirements, the format of citations and the list of references, and other important matters. Select two journals, read the information to prospective contributors carefully, and compare the instructions.

3) Many of you have probably had experiences writing *eisakubun,* personal journals, diaries, and imaginative stories. Compare one of these forms of writing with the general characteristics of academic writing which are described in this chapter. Name the differences.

この章のまとめ

アカデミックライティングを始めとする「学術目的の英語 EAP」は，大学が研究機関であり，また学術コミュニティ（academic community）の中で活動する限り，必ず身につけておかなければならないものである．この章では特に EAP の中でも，専門課程を念頭に置いた全学教育課程（教養課程）での「一般学術目的の英語 English for General Academic Purposes（EGAP）」を説明した．今後の章では，アカデミックライティングのより具体的な側面や技術について紹介していく．

用語説明

a) dissertation
学位のための論文の中で，主に博士号取得のための論文のことを指す．日本語では「学位（請求）論文」と呼ばれることが多い．なお，卒業論文（学士）や修士論文（修士）のことはthesisと呼ばれる．

b) English as a Foreign Language (EFL)
外国語として学習する英語のことである．「外国語として」という表現には，日常語として英語を使用する機会がないことが含意されている．対比される言葉としてEnglish as a Second Language（ESL）があり，こちらは日常生活の中の言葉として学ぶ英語のことを指す．

Chapter 2
Understanding the Structure of Research Papers

Abstract

The main purpose of this chapter is to help students write as well as read a research paper, which is one particular genre of academic writing. A typical research paper, especially in the fields of sciences, consists of four main sections: Introduction, Method, Results, and Discussion (IMRD). The chapter explains how a genre analysis of texts reveals that introductions have components known as *"moves,"* each with a distinct function. This chapter reports the results of a research project (Tajino et al., 2008) which carried out a genre analysis on the introductions of 180 research papers from six disciplines using a CARS model (Swales, 2004), as well as a genre analysis on the titles of 600 papers. Through an understanding of the discussion of the findings of this research project, we hope students will continue to study, on their own, the structure of research papers so that they may learn how to develop logical arguments and write interpretative discussions for their own research papers.

Keywords

Academic discipline, CARS model, Genre, Genre analysis, Move, Step

この章のねらい

一口にアカデミックライティングと言っても，その種類は多岐に渡る．この章ではもっとも中心となる学術論文について紹介する．学術論文はあらゆる分野で共通の性質を持っているのだろうか．ここでは，新たにジャンル（genre）という概念を紹介し，ジャンルによってどのような違いがあるのかを確認する．特に着目するのは，学術論文のタイトルとイントロダクションの議論の展開パターンである．ムーブ（move）と呼ばれるまとまりの繋げ方は，ジャンルによってどのような性質を示しているのだろうか．

1. Introduction

It seems that the research paper is most studied among the academic writing genres familiar to most university students; namely, essay writing, term papers, laboratory reports, grant proposals, and dissertations (e.g., Nwogu, 1997; Swales, 1990). According to the Oxford Dictionary of English (Soanes & Stevenson, 2005, p. 722), the notion of *"genre"* in general is defined as "a style or category of art, music, or literature." In the EAP context, however, Hyland's explanation of genre, which is based on Swales' (1990) extensive discussions of genre, is broadly accepted: "a class of communicative events linked by shared purposes recognized by the members of a particular community" (2002, p. 17).

How can we relate this definition of genre to your needs? In this book the reading and writing of research papers are the "communicative events." "The members of the particular community" are the people who belong to the discourse community interested in a particular research field that a particular paper is part of, and the "shared purposes" are to allow new research to be critically evaluated by the discourse community.

Academic writing textbooks for university students introduce macro-level information about the typical section by section organization of a research paper; e.g., introduction, methodology, results and discussion. You will find this information helpful; however, micro-level information about how central arguments of research reports should be developed within each section is also very important. From the writers' (as well as the readers') points of view, micro-level information about writing structure may be of practical help for students who have had little experience with academic writing. EAP genre analysis research can provide us with more detailed, useful information about the micro-level structural organization of research papers.

2. Move analysis

The notions of "move" and "step" (e.g., Swales, 1990) will be particularly useful in helping you learn about the structure of research articles. The term "move" refers to a component of a paper that serves a particular communicative function and purpose. For example, if part of the text in an *Introduction* section of a paper is a single unit because it describes the work in the paper, it would be identified as a "move." One "move" may consist of smaller units called "steps." If part of the "move" that describes the work in the paper states an outcome of the research, that part is referred to as one "step" of the "move."

Swales's (2004) "Create-A-Research-Space" (CARS) model describes three moves: Move 1 is "establishing a territory," Move 2 is "establishing a niche," and Move 3 is "presenting the present work."

1) Move 1 has a step for "introducing and reviewing items of previous research in the area" (Swales & Feak, 1994, p. 244) which may be identified by signals such as "*Recently* there has been *considerable* interest in … " (Swales, 1990, p. 162).
2) Move 2 includes a step for "indicating a gap in the previous research, or … extending previous knowledge" (Swales & Feak, 1994, p. 244) which may be signaled by an expression such as *"Yet* there is a *dearth* of information" (Swales, 1990, p. 162).
3) Move 3 begins with a step, "announcing present work descriptively and/or purposively" (Swales, 2004, pp. 230–232). Signals of this step include *"The present work* extends the use of the last model to …" (Swales & Feak, 1994, p. 264).

Thus, move analysis can contribute to a better understanding of how research articles are logically constructed. Moreover, by identifying typical expressions which are used in certain moves and steps, move analysis provides you with examples of English expressions which will be useful in your own writing. Improvements in your ability to read and write research papers may result from an understanding of the CARS model for an analytical reading of research articles.

In order to offer practical support for you to improve your writing skills, we will look at some examples of move analysis of two research paper components, which may be called sub-genres: the *Introduction* section and the *Title*.

2.1 The *Introduction* section

Among the sub-genres of a research article, the *Introduction* section is considered to be one of the most difficult to write because it plays a crucial role in attracting readers by explaining the significance of the research to its discourse community (e.g., Swales, 1990, 2004). Therefore, an understanding of the *Introduction* section would be of a great help for students in EGAP academic writing courses.

Many of the previous genre studies on the *Introduction* section, however, have delineated the *Introduction* structure of papers from only one discipline each. The study we will present in this chapter (Tajino et al., 2008) conducted an analysis of *Introductions* using a 3.7 million-word research paper corpus (600 articles) in six academic disciplines: sociology, education, economics, medicine, pharmacology, and engineering. The *Introductions* were analyzed by means of Swales's CARS model which describes three moves and several steps, as noted previously.

2.1.1 Move patterns across six disciplines

The results of the study, in which a total of 180 *Introductions* from ten articles randomly selected from three journals from each of six disciplines were examined, were as follows:

1) The pattern of "Move 1 → Move 2 → Move 3" was found in 50.0% of the cases in sociology, 6.7% in education, 30.0% in economics, 30.0% in medicine, 60.0% in pharmacology, and 36.7% in engineering. Patterns that included "Move 1 → Move 2 → Move 3" in different combinations (e.g., Move 1 → Move 3 → Move 1 → Move 2 → Move 3) were found in 23.3% of the cases in sociology, 60.0% in education, 43.3% in economics, 40.0% in medicine, 10.0% in pharmacology, and 50.0% in engineering.

It should be noted that even within a single discipline, there were distinct differences in move patterns. In the field of economics, for example, in a comparison of the *Journal of Economic Theory* and the *Journal of Political Economy*, the pattern of "Move 1 → Move 2 → Move 3" was found in 60.0% of the articles in the former journal, whereas this pattern was not found at all in the latter.

2) The recursive pattern of "Move 1 → Move 2" (i.e., Move 2 → Move 1) was not found in any articles in pharmacology, whereas it was found in 6.7% of the cases in sociology, 10.0% in education, 10.0% in economics, 40.0% in medicine, and 30.0% in engineering.
3) There were *Introductions* that did not include Move 2; i.e., Move 2 was not found in 16.7% of the cases in sociology, 13.3% in education, 13.3% in economics, 10.0% in medicine, 20.0% in pharmacology, and 3.3% in engineering.

2.1.2 The proportion of each move in the *Introduction*

The proportion of each move in the *Introduction* based on the number of words was examined and the results are summarized below. A difference among the disciplines was found in the proportion of each move in the *Introductions*. As Table 2.1 shows, in medicine and pharmacology, Move 1 accounts for more than 70% of the words and Move 3 accounts for more than 60% of the words in economics.

Table 2.1 Proportion of moves in the introductions (%)

Disciplines	Move 1	Move 2	Move 3	Total
Sociology	46.9	13.6	39.5	100
Education	58.9	11.8	29.3	100
Economics	31.4	4.6	64.0	100
Medicine	72.1	10.4	17.5	100
Pharmacology	74.0	9.5	16.5	100
Engineering	41.4	15.8	42.8	100

To summarize the findings listed above, despite some variations among disciplines, the pattern of "Move 1→Move 2→Move 3" was used in all disciplines. It was also shown that variations might occur within a single discipline. This might be attributed to the differences in research conventions and to differences in the discourse community (see Ozturk, 2007).

2.2 The *Titles*

Previous studies suggest that the *Titles* may vary according to discipline (see, for example, Anthony, 2001; Haggan, 2004; Soler, 2007). Our analysis included 600 titles from six disciplines which were analyzed in terms of linguistic structure and vocabulary.

2.2.1 Structural patterns of the *Titles*

According to Soler (2007), *Titles* can be classified as follows:

1) Nominal-group construction
    e.g., "The significance of team teaching in Japanese EFL contexts"
2) Full-sentence construction
    e.g., "Team teaching makes a difference in Japanese EFL contexts"
3) Compound construction
    e.g., "Team teaching in Japanese EFL contexts: Does it make a difference?"

Table 2.2 Structural patterns of the Titles[1] (number of titles)

	Single construction		Compound construction	Total
	Nominal-group	Full-sentence		
Sociology	36	1	63	100
Education	41	6	53	100
Economics	72	0	28	100
Medicine	42	51	7	100
Pharmacology	50	33	17	100
Engineering	88	0	12	100

As the table shows, the titles varied according to discipline. For example, in economics, pharmacology, and engineering, more than half of the titles were categorized as nominal-group construction; whereas in sociology and education, the compound construction type accounted for over half of the titles. In contrast, in medicine, the full-sentence construction type was employed most often. It was also observed that the full-sentence construction type was typically used in medicine and pharmacology, and the compound construction type was used in a relatively large number of titles in three disciplines: sociology, education, and economics.

The findings also indicated that even within the same structure there were some disciplinary differences. For example, the compound construction titles, in sociology, education, and economics, sometimes employed "interrogative" forms. The following example of a title from an economics article was typical of interrogative titles: "Do boards affect performance? Evidence from corporate restructuring" (Perry & Shivdasani, 2005). In contrast, in the science disciplines (i.e., medicine, pharmacology, and engineering) interrogative forms were not used.

The same was true for the full-sentence construction type. Titles in medicine and pharmacology were always in "affirmative" forms, whereas in education four out of six full-sentence titles were interrogative as in "Are young children's drawings canonically biased?" (as in Picard & Durand's 2005 title).

2.2.2 Vocabulary used in the *Titles*

Analysis from a vocabulary perspective provided additional comparisons of differences in titles according to discipline. Several words or phrases tended to appear in certain disciplines, yet only in specific structures. For example, in the nominal-group construction and in the compound construction titles, the word *revisit* appeared in all disciplines once, or more than once, in the form of the past participle *revisited* or the gerund *revisiting* as in an engineering paper entitled "Control of macro-micro manipulators revisited" (Parsa, Angeles, & Misra, 2005). In addition, in 84 compound construction titles, which were typically used in medicine and pharmacology, certain words e.g., *regulate* and *require* frequently appeared.

Certain words or phrases were used in a particular discipline regardless of title structure. For example, in sociology, four titles began with *toward(s)*; however, the use of *toward(s)* was not found in the titles in the other disciplines. In engineering papers, the word *analysis* was used in nine titles; however, this word occurred only once in medicine and not at all in pharmacology. In medicine and pharmacology, titles seemed to directly reflect the results of the research. In other words, the titles seemed to indicate a product-oriented approach, whereas in engineering the titles tended to indicate a process-oriented approach, for example, by referring to an analysis or an experiment.

The number and types of words used in the titles were also studied. Table 2.3 and Table 2.4 present the average number of words and the vocabulary category of the words in the titles[2].

Table 2.3 Average number of words in the titles

Disciplines	Sociology	Education	Economics	Medicine	Pharmacology	Engineering
Mean	10.7	11.6	8.7	12.6	14.2	10.9
SD	4.3	3.8	3.8	4.4	5.4	3.7

Table 2.4 Vocabulary: types of words in the titles (%)

Disciplines	General words	Academic words	Technical words	Total
Sociology	63.5	17.2	19.3	100
Education	65.4	15.0	19.6	100
Economics	62.1	18.2	19.7	100
Medicine	44.6	12.1	43.3	100
Pharmacology	41.2	10.3	48.5	100
Engineering	53.4	17.2	29.4	100

Table 2.3 shows that titles in science (particularly in medicine and pharmacology) contain more words. As Table 2.4 shows, many words used in the titles of research papers in any of the disciplines can be categorized as general words; however, in science (particularly in medicine and pharmacology) technical words represent more than 40% of the words in the title. From these results, it is possible to argue that the titles in science describe the paper's contents and results in specific terms. However, titles in other disciplines use fewer words which are more often in the general word category. Different expectations of different discourse communities may determine the type of title.

3. Conclusion

In this chapter we have seen how analyses of the *Introduction* sections and the *Titles* of research papers reveal some common patterns among disciplines and some important differences. Future research will likely usefully deepen our understanding of the structure of research papers. Students are advised to find the regularities of texts by themselves (Swales & Feak, 2004). In other words, we recommend that you look carefully for patterns in structure and in vocabulary. If you understand how, and for what purposes, research articles in your field are structured, especially at the less obvious micro-level, this knowledge of the writing conventions used in your field will help you read research articles. Moreover, when you begin to do your own research, you will be able to write it up in the style accepted by your discourse community.

References

Anthony, L. (2001). Characteristic features of research article titles in computer science. *IEEE transactions on professional communication, 44,* 187–194.

Coxhead, A. (2000). A new academic word list. *TESOL Quarterly, 34*(2), 213–238.

Haggan, M. (2004). Research paper titles in literature, linguistics and science: Dimensions of attraction. *Journal of Pragmatics, 36*(2), 293–317.

Hyland, K. (2002). Genre: Language, context, and literacy. *Annual Review of Applied Linguistics, 22,* 113–135.

Nwogu, K.N. (1997). The medical research paper: Structures and functions. *English for Specific Purposes, 16*(2), 119–137.

Ozturk, I. (2007). The textual organisation of research article introductions in applied linguistics: Variability within a single discipline. *English for Specific Purposes, 26*(1), 25–38.

Parsa, K., Angeles, J., & Misra, A. K. (2005). Control of macro-micro manipulators revisited. *Journal of Dynamic Systems, Measurement, and Control, 127,* 688–699.

Perry, T., & Shivdasani, A. (2005). Do boards affect performance? Evidence from corporate restructuring. *Journal of Business, 78,* 1403–1431.

Picard, D., & Durand, K. (2005). Are young children's drawings canonically biased? *Journal of Experimental Child Psychology, 90,* 48–64.

Soanes, C., & Stevenson, A. (Eds.) (2005). *The Oxford Dictionary of English* (2nd ed.). Oxford: Oxford University Press.

Soler, V. (2007). Writing titles in science: An exploratory study. *English for Specific Purposes, 26*(1), 90–102.

Swales, J. M. (1990). *Genre analysis: English in academic and research settings.* Cambridge: Cambridge University Press.

Swales, J. M. (2004). *Research genres: Exploration and applications.* Cambridge: Cambridge University Press.

Swales, J. M., & Feak, C. B. (1994). *Academic writing for graduate students: A course for nonnative speakers of English.* Ann Arbor: University of Michigan Press.

Swales, J. M., & Feak, C. B. (2004). *Academic writing for graduate students: Essential tasks and skills. (2nd ed.).* Ann Arbor: University of Michigan Press.

Tajino, A., Terauchi, H., Kanamaru, T., Maswana, S., & Yamada, H. (2008). *Eigo gakujyutsu ronbun shippitsu no tame no kyozai kaihatsu ni mukete–ronbun kopasu no kouchiku to oyou* [Toward the development of English academic writing materials: The creation and application of a research paper-based corpus in six academic disciplines], *Kyoto University Researches in Higher Education, 14,* 111–121.

West, M. (1953). *A general service list of English words.* London: Longmans, Green and Co.

Notes

1. "Single construction" refers to a title consisting of one noun phrase or sentence, while "compound construction" refers to a title consisting of more than one phrase or sentence combined with a colon.
2. Vocabulary was classified into three categories: general words, academic words, and technical words. The term "general words" means the words listed in General Service List (West, 1953); "academic words" refers to the words listed in the Academic Word List (Coxhead, 2000); and "technical words" are words which were not included in either list.

Learning Tasks

1) Select five research articles in one field that you are interested in. Use the information in this chapter to analyze the *Titles* according to type of vocabulary and structural pattern.

2) Select one research article and use the information in this chapter to conduct a "move" analysis on the *Introduction* section.

3) Select one research article in each of any three different academic disciplines. Use the criteria from this chapter to compare the *Titles* and *Introduction* sections.

この章のまとめ

学術論文は大きな構造とそれを構成する小さな構造から成り立っていることが理解できただろうか．イントロダクションという大きな構造は，ムーブと呼ばれる，より小さなレベルの構造によって構成され，その構造はCARSモデルと呼ばれるパターンを構成するのが規範的とされる．ただし，このムーブのパターンは専門分野によって微妙に異なるため，専門分野の特徴をよく知っておくことも重要である．同じように，タイトルの性質も専門分野ごとに違いがあるので注意しておこう．

用語説明

a) grant proposal
学術研究のために，国（政府機関）や民間の財団などから交付される研究補助金のことをグラント（grant）と呼ぶことがある．グラントを獲得するためには，研究者が自らの研究を説明する申請書（grant proposal）を提出しなければならないことが多い．

b) discourse community
ESPやEAPの文脈の中では，特定の大学（学部・学科）や特定の専門分野の学術研究会などの特定の専門家集団のことを指す．こうした専門家集団においては，構成員は共通の概念や目標を共有しているものと考えられる．

Chapter 3
Academic Vocabulary and Academic Writing

Abstract

This chapter discusses the role of academic vocabulary knowledge in academic writing with a brief review of the literature on EFL vocabulary learning and teaching. Important questions are addressed such as What does "knowing a word" mean? and How many English words do native speakers of English and Japanese university students know? In approaching these questions, key concepts related to the forms of vocabulary knowledge, such as its "receptive" and "productive" aspects, are introduced with exemplary learning tasks so that the nature of vocabulary knowledge may be better understood. Due to the great number of English words which may be classified as academic words, students must necessarily make decisions about which words to spend their time learning first. Thus, samples of words which are featured in the three academic word lists of the Kyoto University Academic Vocabulary Database are also provided.

Keywords

Academic vocabulary, Kyoto University Academic Vocabulary Database, Receptive and productive vocabulary, Vocabulary knowledge

この章のねらい

アカデミックライティングにおいては，文のスタイルだけでなく，そこで使用される語彙についても，一般的なものとは異なった性質を持つ．この章ではアカデミックライティングと語彙知識との関係について見ていく．ある語彙の知識を持っているというのは，どのような状態を指すのだろうか．また，その語彙の数はどのように測ればよいのだろうか．そして，どのような語彙を学習すればよいのだろうか．語彙とライティングの関係について着目しながら，読み進めてほしい．

1. Introduction

As discussed in Chapter 1, academic vocabulary is a defining feature of academic writing. For example, if you need to write an in-class essay for a general audience on the issue of climate change, but you just cannot remember the expression for *solar energy*, what will happen? You might rely on your strategic skills and paraphrase it by using an alternative expression such as "energy produced from sunshine." Paraphrasing will help you make your communication successful in some situations. Yet, this is not true in every case. Some words referred to as jargon, words used by one certain group or profession, or the specialized words of certain fields of study (e.g., *cochlea* and *glutamate*) would not be easy to efficiently paraphrase. Certain words which are rarely used in our daily conversation but quite frequently used in a certain register, a variety of language used for a particular purpose, can be used to show that you are a member of a certain group and that you know the group's special vocabulary and the other ways in which the members communicate with one another.

The roles that vocabulary knowledge plays in academic writing have been the subject of a great deal of research in recent years. A review of the literature of vocabulary learning and teaching reveals that questions like *What does "knowing a word" mean?* and *How many English words do Japanese university students know?* are among the fundamental matters that researchers have explored. We will also provide samples of words which are featured in the academic word lists of the Kyoto University Academic Vocabulary Database.

2. Academic vocabulary and academic writing

2.1 The significance of vocabulary knowledge

It is often claimed that vocabulary knowledge is essential for the development of language proficiency and "of concern to all four language skills" (Jordan, 1997, p. 149). It seems that "words are the basic building blocks of language, the units of meaning from which larger structures such as sentences, paragraphs and whole texts are formed" (Read, 2000, p. 1).

Without vocabulary knowledge or without recognizing a word *as a word*, it would not be easy to interpret a message simply by listening to a sound sequence.

Research on the relationship between text coverage (i.e., the percentage of running words in the text known by the readers) and reading comprehension for non-native speakers of English suggests that 98% text coverage in a fiction text is necessary for successful comprehension (Nation, 2006). If this is true, in the case of a non-fiction text, at least the same percentage of text coverage is likely to be necessary. It should be noted that the 98% of fiction text coverage would require about an 8,000–9,000 word-family vocabulary (Nation, 2006). Note that a "word family" can be defined as "a base word with its inflections and derivatives *(stimulate + stimulated, stimulates, stimulating, stimulation, stimulant,* and *stimulative)"* (Schmitt & McCarthy, 1997, p. 331).

It can be reasonably assumed that vocabulary knowledge is likely equally important for the development of academic writing skills.

2.2 The role of academic vocabulary in academic writing

A review of the literature on EFL vocabulary learning and teaching shows that the appropriate use of English vocabulary is considered to be one of the most difficult aspects of writing for non-native English speaking graduate students (Shaw, 1991). For example, in your course reports at university you are expected to avoid using the English conjunction *so,* although you can use it in casual conversation with your classmates; in academic writing, expressions such as *hence, therefore,* and *as a consequence* are considered appropriate substitutes.

Leki and Carson (1994) claim that expanding vocabulary knowledge is one of the most frequently expressed needs of undergraduates in English-as-a-Second-Language (ESL) writing courses. It was reported that students' lexical errors were regarded as the error which had the most serious negative effect on teachers' assessments of student writing (see Santos, 1988). Other studies have demonstrated a strong correlation between error-free lexical variation and holistic writing test scores (e.g., Engber, 1995).

You may deepen your understanding of the crucial role of academic vocabulary knowledge through translation tasks. The following paragraph illustrates the challenge. Translate it into English, paying careful attention to the need to find suitable English equivalents for the specialized, academic words which are underlined in the passage.

「今回我々は，発生中のラットの蝸牛にある支持細胞が自発的にATPを放出し，これが周辺の内有毛細胞を脱分極してグルタミン酸を放出させ，一次聴覚ニューロンに不連続な活動電位のバーストを生じさせることを明らかにする．」(Tritsch, Yi, Gale, Glowatzki, & Bergles, 2007, pp. 50–55)[1].

3. What do we mean by "knowing a word"?

We have so far discussed the significance of academic vocabulary knowledge in academic writing. Yet, what does "knowing a word" mean? Is it possible to claim that you know the word *eradicate,* if you can answer the following multiple-choice question correctly?

> *In spite of unprecedented efforts by most of the world's intergovernmental organizations to eradicate extreme poverty, much aid money is not used as intended.*
>   a. suppress
>   b. get an estimate of
>   c. get rid of
>   d. reduce

You would probably agree with Nation (2001) that knowing a word includes knowledge about:

1) how the word is pronounced and spelled;
2) what meaning can be expressed by what form of the word; and
3) in what patterns, and with what other words, the word occurs.

Thus, as Table 3.1 shows, vocabulary knowledge includes the three aspects: "form," "meaning," and "use."

Table 3.1 Aspects of vocabulary knowledge

form （形式）	spoken　発音
	written　綴り
	word parts　語の構成要素
meaning （意味）	form and meaning 語形と意味のつながり
	concept and referents 概念と指示物
	associations　連想
use （使用）	grammatical function 文法的機能
	collocations　コロケーション
	constraints on use 使用時の制約

Furthermore, each aspect can be discussed from two different perspectives: receptive and productive vocabulary knowledge. Receptive vocabulary knowledge is related to comprehending meaning from a particular word form in reading and listening, while productive vocabulary knowledge is related to conveying meaning by using an appropriate word form in writing and speaking (Nation, 2001).

3.1　Receptive vocabulary knowledge

The following task will serve to clarify the meaning of receptive vocabulary knowledge. Give the Japanese equivalent of the underlined word:

> *The 2008 economic crisis nearly led to a* <u>meltdown</u> *of the global financial system.*

If you can understand the meaning of *meltdown* in the context of this sentence, you have receptive knowledge of the word, as it is used in one special sense, in the example sentence. However, if you do not think you would be able to use *meltdown* in the same sense in your own speech or in your own writing, you cannot claim to have productive knowledge of *meltdown*.

3.2 Productive vocabulary knowledge

The following challenge is an example of the meaning of productive vocabulary knowledge. Write in the missing word that starts with the three letters *"ant."* You will have to do a word search based on what you understand of the rest of the two sentences and also on your memory list of words that begin with the letters "ant" and, then, produce the correct word.

> *Hence, similar results were ant_____ from male and female informants in the study. Very different findings had not been expected.*

In general, as far as EFL learners' vocabulary size is concerned, receptive knowledge is likely to be larger than productive knowledge (e.g., Melka, 1997). For the purpose of improving your academic writing skills, you should make efforts to develop your productive vocabulary knowledge.

4. How many English words do we know?

4.1 Native speakers of English

Research suggests that educated native speakers of English know about 20,000 *word families* (Nation, 2006). As noted above, a word family covers a base word with its inflections and derivatives. If the derivatives of the 20,000 word families are counted as separate words, the number of known words would be much higher. Aitchison (2003, p. 7) states that "the number of words which an educated adult native speaker of English knows, and can potentially use, is unlikely to be less than 50,000, and may be much higher."

4.2 Japanese university students

How many English words do you think you know? Research suggests that the average vocabulary size of Japanese university students is from 2,300 to 3,700–including knowledge of derivatives but not counting the number of known inflections (Mochizuki, Aizawa, & Tono, 2003); i.e., the word *stimulation* is a derivative of the base word *stimulate* and they are counted as two separate words; however, *stimulates* is an inflected form of the base word *stimulate* and these two words are counted as one word, not two separate words. If this is the case, Japanese students' vocabulary size is considerably smaller than the native speakers' vocabulary of 50,000 words. This gap should not be disregarded; however, we will show that it is a gap that can be narrowed sufficiently to allow university students to competently read and write research papers.

5. Academic vocabulary: EGAP vocabulary and ESAP vocabulary

Academic vocabulary refers to a group of words that appears frequently and widely in academic texts, while rarely used in non-academic texts, such as friendly e-mails to your close friends about weekend plans (see Coxhead, 2000; Martin, 1976). In this chapter, academic vocabulary will be considered in an EAP framework (see Chapter 1); i.e., EGAP vocabulary and ESAP vocabulary. EGAP vocabulary refers to a group of words that is common across different fields or disciplines, whereas ESAP vocabulary refers to a group of words that is specific to one particular field or discipline. These two categories of words may be equivalent to words usually referred to as "academic words" and "technical words" respectively (see Nation, 2001). Note that in the literature of vocabulary learning and teaching, different terms have often been used to identify categories of words which are similar or the same. For example, "technical vocabulary" (e.g., Chung & Nation, 2003; Coxhead & Nation, 2001) has received numerous labels, such as "specialist vocabulary" (Kennedy & Bolitho, 1984), "specialized lexis" (Baker, 1988), "technical terms" (Yang, 1986), and "technical words" (Farrell, 1990). These terms, from an EAP-curriculum perspective, may be categorized as "ESAP vocabulary."

In a survey of academic texts, Nation (2001) found that a vocabulary size of the most frequent 2,000 words in English made up 78.2% of the texts, and words from Coxhead's Academic Word List (2000) were 8.5% of the words, and 13.3% of the words were from outside of these two lists. Note that the Academic Word List is claimed to contain 570 word families that can account for approximately 10.0% of the total words in academic texts from four disciplines: arts, commerce, law, and science (Coxhead, 2000). To get an approximate measure of the vocabulary challenge in academic research papers, we could make an extrapolation from Nation's data and estimate that the proportion of EGAP and ESAP words used in a typical academic paper might be as follows: EGP vocabulary (78.2%); EGAP vocabulary (8.5%); and others, including ESAP vocabulary (13.3%), (see Figure 3.1). It is important to conduct research to confirm this, yet for our purposes in this chapter, it is important to note that most, if not all, of the most frequent 2,000 words in English should be known by students who successfully complete the high school English course in Japan. Thus, the vocabulary learning challenge is not beyond the reach of students who are determined to learn the English words used in their research fields.

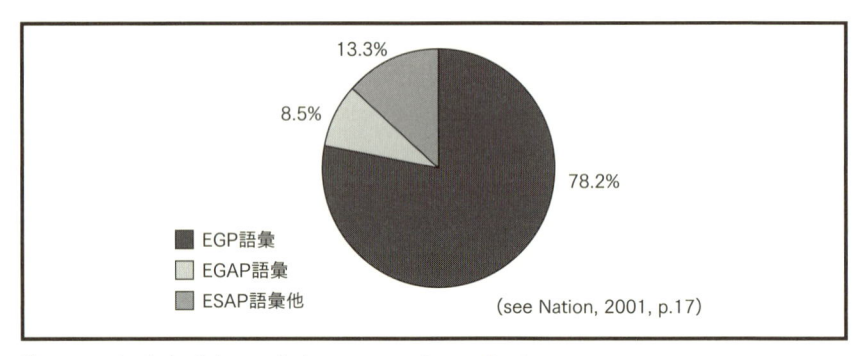

Figure 3.1 Analysis of the vocabulary content of an academic text

As shown in Figure 3.1, EGAP vocabulary, as a percentage of the total number of words is rather small. However, quantitative data only, which may not reflect any qualitative aspect of the vocabulary, is shown in the figure. EGAP vocabulary deserves considerable attention for at least two reasons: 1) the quality of the contribution made to an academic paper by EGAP vocabulary is important; and 2) because this comparatively small group of words is central to the expression of the fundamental messages of research articles, the vocabulary learning challenge is manageable. Furthermore, ESAP vocabulary (13.3%, or less, of the total) is expected to be learned at a later stage (e.g., at the postgraduate level). Read (2000, p. 159) states, "Specialised vocabulary [referred to as ESAP vocabulary in this chapter] is likely to be better acquired through content instruction by a subject teacher than through language teaching." If this is the case, an important challenge is to find ways to add EGAP vocabulary to undergraduate students' English vocabulary knowledge.

6. The Kyoto University Academic Vocabulary Database

As can be concluded from the discussion above, vocabulary education is a central concern in the development of an EAP curriculum at a multidisciplinary research university in Japan. Furthermore, vocabulary education is important since the vocabulary size of Japanese university students tends to decrease in the years after they pass the entrance examinations (see Okamoto, 2005). With these issues in mind, at Kyoto University, vocabulary education was planned from an EAP-curriculum perspective; and three types of interdisciplinary data-based academic word lists were compiled (see Appendix 1 for an outline of this project: the *Kyoto University Data-based List of 1,110 Essential Academic Words*). Sample words from the word lists are shown in Tables 3.2 (EGAP word list), 3.3 (EGAP-A word list for Arts majors), and 3.4 (EGAP-S word list for Sciences majors). How many words on each word list do you think you know and can use appropriately?

Table 3.2 EGAP word list

function	range	cell	imply	factor
potential	consistent	assumption	individual	region
feature	equation	indicate	issue	correspond
hence	variable	contrast	hypothesis	conclusion
significant	strategy	previous	culture	involve
procedure	outcome	construct	estimate	context
reveal	reference	interaction	demonstrate	definition
conduct	distribution	parameter	phase	derive

Table 3.3 EGAP-A word list

treaty	doctrine	enforcement	governance	jurisdiction
congress	grant	radical	judicial	causal
clause	quote	cite	narrative	legitimacy
directive	statute	plea	charter	sovereignty
executive	scope	prosecutor	avatar	dispute
impose	ibid	payoff	legislative	asset
liability	breach	defendant	stakeholder	alliance
draft	tribunal	coalition	ideological	plaintiff

Table 3.4 EGAP-S word list

protein	chromosome	shear	blot	telomere
cancer	interval	plot	antibody	concentration
atom	solvent	strain	constant	transcription
input	assay	dose	amino	deformation
mutation	neuron	magnetic	ligand	receptor
tissue	plasmid	lipid	component	plasma
pulse	gradient	membrane	linear	genome
crystal	substrate	purify	pathway	mortality

7. Conclusion

We have discussed the roles of vocabulary knowledge in academic writing with a brief review of the literature of EFL vocabulary learning and teaching. In so doing, we addressed important questions for vocabulary learning for general purposes such as *What does "knowing a word" mean?* and *How many English words do native speakers of English and Japanese university students know?* More importantly, we have introduced the fundamental concepts of EGAP and ESAP vocabulary and information about the first corpus-based EGAP word lists prepared especially for

Japanese-speaking university students. The three word lists (i.e., the EGAP, the EGAP-A, and the EGAP-S word lists) will help you identify the academic words which you should learn first when you try to build your vocabulary.

We hope that you have a better understanding of the nature of vocabulary knowledge after reading this chapter and completing the learning tasks. We have seen that vocabulary knowledge involves at least three aspects: form, meaning, and use, each with receptive and productive knowledge. Before you go on, ask yourself one essential question: Which aspects of vocabulary knowledge should I develop further to improve my own writing skills for academic purposes?

References

Aitchison, J. (2003). *Words in the mind: An introduction to the mental lexicon.* (3rd ed.) Oxford: Blackwell.

Baker, M. (1988). Sub-technical vocabulary and the ESP teacher: An analysis of some rhetorical items in medical journal articles. *Reading in a Foreign Language, 64*(2), 91–105.

Chung, T. M., & Nation, I. S. P. (2003). Technical vocabulary in specialised texts. *Reading in a Foreign Language, 15*(2), 102–116.

Coxhead, A. (2000). A new academic word list. *TESOL Quarterly, 34*(2), 213–238.

Coxhead, A., & Nation, P. (2001). The specialized vocabulary of English for academic purposes. In J. Flowerdew & M. Peacock (Eds.), Research perspectives on English for academic purposes (pp. 252–267). Cambridge: Cambridge University Press.

Engber, C. (1995). The relationship of lexical proficiency and the quality of ESL compositions. *Journal of Second Language Writing, 4*(2), 139–155.

Farrell, P. (1990). Vocabulary in ESP: A lexical analysis of the English of electronics and a study of semi-technical vocabulary. *CLCS Occasional Paper,* No. 25, Trinity College.

Jordan, R. R. (1997). *English for academic purposes: A guide and resource book for teachers.* Cambridge: Cambridge University Press.

Kennedy, C., & Bolitho, R. (1984). *English for specific purposes.* London: Macmillan.

Kyoto University EAP Vocabulary Research Group and Kenkyusha (2009). *Kyodai Gakujutsugoi Deitabeisu Kihon Eitango 1110.* [Kyoto University Data-based List of 1,110 Essential Academic Words.], Tokyo: Kenkyusha.

Leki, I., & Carson, J. (1994). Students' perceptions of EAP writing instruction and writing needs across the disciplines. *TESOL Quarterly, 28*(1), 81–101.

Martin, A. (1976). Teaching academic vocabulary to foreign graduate students. *TESOL Quarterly, 10*(1), 91–97.

Melka, F. (1997). Receptive vs. productive aspects of vocabulary. In N. Schmitt & M. McCarthy (Eds.), *Vocabulary: Description, acquisition, and pedagogy* (pp. 84–102). Cambridge: Cambridge University Press.

Mochizuki, M., Aizawa, K., & Tono, Y. (2003). *Eigo goi no shido manyuaru*. [Teaching manual of English vocabulary.], Tokyo: Taisyukan shoten.

Nation, I. S. P. (2001). *Learning vocabulary in another language.* Cambridge: Cambridge University Press.

Nation, I. S. P. (2006). How large a vocabulary is needed for reading and listening? *The Canadian Modern Language Review, 63*(1), 59–82.

Okamoto, M. (2005). *University students' lexical acquisition and attrition in English as a foreign language.* Unpublished MA thesis. Kyoto University.

Read, J. (2000). *Assessing vocabulary.* Cambridge: Cambridge University Press.

Santos, T. (1988). Professors' reactions to the academic writing of nonnative-speaking students. *TESOL Quarterly, 22*(1), 69–90.

Schmitt, N., & McCarthy, M. (Eds.). (1997). *Vocabulary: Description, acquisition and pedagogy.* Cambridge: Cambridge University Press.

Shaw, P. (1991). Science research students' composing processes. *English for Specific Purposes, 10*(3), 189–206.

Tritsch, N. X., Yi, E., Gale, J. E., Glowatzki, E., & Bergles, D. E. (2007). The origin of spontaneous activity in the developing auditory system. *Nature, 450*(1), 50–55.

West, M. (1953). *A general service list of English words.* London: Longmans, Green and Co.

Yang, H. (1986). A new technique for identifying scientific/technical terms and describing science texts. *Literary and Linguistic Computing, 1*(2), 93–103.

Note

1   *Translation Task:* The excerpt is from the abstract of an article originally published in English in the journal *Nature* 450, 50–51(1 November 2007), and translated for the Japanese language version of the journal. The title of the article is "The origin of spontaneous activity in the developing auditory system." [Original in English: "Here we show that supporting cells in the developing rat cochlea spontaneously release ATP, which causes nearby inner hair cells to depolarize and release glutamate, triggering discrete bursts of action potentials in primary auditory neurons."]

Answer Key

1) p.36 Multiple-choice question: C
2) p.38 Fill-in-the Blank question: anticipated

Appendix 1

An outline of the steps taken to establish the academic vocabulary database and the three EGAP word lists:

1) The Dean of each faculty nominated English-language research journals which were representative of the targets of study and research in the faculty's specialized fields of study.

2) A database of approximately 10 million words was compiled from a selection of 1,700 research papers from 170 journals; EGP words included in West's (1953) General Service List were eliminated from the database.
3) Research articles were selected randomly from each of the journals recommended to compile the database. The database was separated into three categories: words common to both Arts and Sciences (the EGAP word list), words found in Arts only (the EGAP-A word list), and words found in Sciences only (the EGAP-S word list). The database in each category was reduced by range and frequency statistical procedures to 2,000 words.
4) University EAP teachers reduced the 2,000 words in each category to a total of 1,110 words in all three categories by taking into account the needs of the students in their EAP courses. The usefulness of the selected words was verified by confirming their use in research journals which had not been used to compile the database.
5) *Kenkyusha,* a leading dictionary publisher in Japan, added definitions and example phrases or sentences in English. University EAP teachers reviewed and revised the definitions and examples. *The Kyodai Gakujutsugoi Deitabeisu Kihon Eitango 1110* (The Kyoto University Data-based List of 1,110 Essential Academic Words) was published in June, 2009.

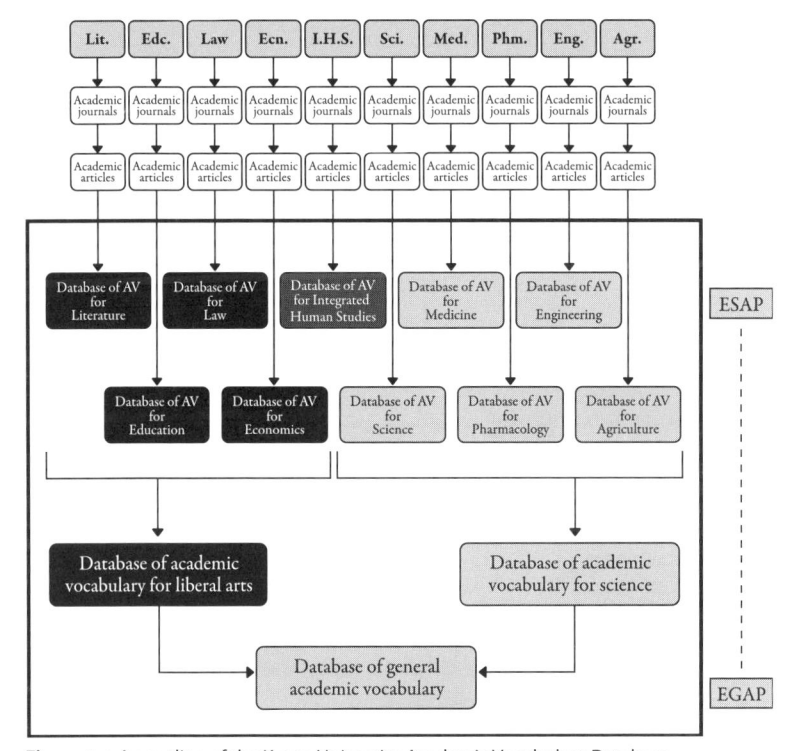

Figure 3.2 An outline of the Kyoto University Academic Vocabulary Database

Learning Tasks

1) Find a research paper in a field that interests you. Read the title, the abstract, and the introduction. Identify the words that you do not understand. Of the total number of words, calculate the percentage of words unfamiliar to you.

2) Make a list of the unknown words from the task mentioned above. Try to learn these words within one week, before your next class. Experiment with different ways to learn these words and see which ways work best for you. Report to the class about which vocabulary learning strategies you used and which strategies you found useful. Check one month later to find out if you can still remember the words. If not, revise your learning strategies.

3) Select the abstract of one research paper from an arts discipline and the abstract of a research paper in a sciences discipline. Calculate the percentage of the total words in each abstract which can be found in the *Kyoto University Data-based List of 1,110 Essential Academic Words*.

4) Words used in life sciences are an important part of EGAP vocabulary. Visit the following website: http://lsd.pharm.kyoto-u.ac.jp/ja/index.html. Prepare to make a short speech to your classmates in which you use at least five of the words you find in the dictionary on the website.

───── この章のまとめ

一般的な大学生の語彙サイズというものが分かっただろうか．学術論文の理解には，専門用語だけではなく，一般学術語彙と呼ばれるあらゆる分野に共通する語彙の知識が必要となる．学術目的の英語のためには，一般的な語彙集だけではなく，学術語彙を集めた語彙集による学習が求められている．

用語説明

a) register
言葉は常に同じように使用されるのではなく，状況や目的に応じた形で用いられる．ある言語が用いられる場面や状況，目的などといった条件や文脈のことを言語使用域（register）という．本書が対象とする言語使用域は，主に学術論文ということになる．

b) inflection and derivative
英語では文法による変化を表す際に，単語の形が変わる．例えば，名詞の複数形に，–(e)sが付いたり，過去形の規則動詞に–(e)dが付いたりして語形が変化する．これを屈折（inflection）と呼ぶ．一方，元となる単語に–tionや–tive, dis–のような接辞が付くことによって，元の単語の品詞などが変わることがある．このような変化を派生（derivation）といい，派生の結果，作られた語のことを派生語（derivative）と呼ぶ．

c) receptive and productive vocabulary
受容語彙と発表語彙．前者は英単語を見たり聞いたりした時にその語の日本語としての意味を知っている語彙を指し，後者はその逆に，日本語の意味から適切な英単語を産出できる語彙のことを指す．発表語彙の数は受容語彙の数の約半分程度という調査結果がある．

d) collocation
何らかの意味的・文法的つながりを持つ単語同士のまとまりのことで，習慣的に使われる語と語の間の共起関係を指す．結びつきやすい語は単語ごとに決まっていることが多い．例えば，同じ液体であっても，oilとteaでは，濃さを表すのに結びつく語がそれぞれ異なる．一般に，前者はthick, 後者はstrongとともに用いられ，それぞれthick oil, strong teaとなる．

Chapter 4
Critical Thinking and Reading Research Papers

Abstract

This chapter begins with a discussion of why reading research papers in English is an important way to build your knowledge base in the academic fields in which you are interested by learning about the connections researchers make between their own research and the relevant work of other researchers. Indeed, the first step in planning research is reading research papers. Learning how to follow the convention of carefully giving credit to the researchers whose work you base your own research on is described as the way young researchers earn membership in research discourse communities. The thinking processes that scholars employ as they carry out research is called "critical thinking." Critical thinking is defined as a way of understanding and evaluating research in order to generate ideas for plans to make your own original research contributions.

Keywords

Academic freedom, Critical reading, Critical thinking skills, Plagiarism, Research discourse community, Scholarly inquiry

この章のねらい

この章では一度，ライティングから離れて，英語学術論文の読み方について説明する．学術研究においては，書くために読むという姿勢が重要になる．そのため，ただ漠然と学術論文を読んでいては意味がない．研究を進めていく上で，学術論文をどのように読んでいくのかを，ここでは紹介する．また，研究上における学術論文の適切な扱い方についても学んでほしい．

1. Introduction

As a student you attend lectures and read in the arts and sciences in your first years at university. The lecturers and the authors prepare their materials by reviewing the literature in their fields, by thinking about how it all fits together, and by forming their own views of what can be done to promote better understandings in their chosen fields of study. You can do something similar yourself once you have a solid understanding of the fundamentals in the areas you want to explore. To establish your own intellectual independence you can begin your life as a researcher by reading research papers and by thinking about what contributions you will try to add. You can turn your dreams of finding a useful place in the university world into reality by conducting your own research activities. By writing research articles, you will give other people opportunities to think about your work. This chapter will discuss the most crucial aspect of your role as a university student: your development as an independent thinker.

In Chapter 1, you read about academic communities, groups of people who share common interests. In this chapter, we will discuss one particular type of academic community, research discourse communities.

2. Reading research papers: Building your knowledge base and finding models for your own writing

Reading reports of research is the primary means of beginning a research project. In other words, in order to learn to write your own research papers, you should read good examples of research reports in your field. There are three practical types of readily available good writing models:

1) The best examples of research reports written in English by your "sempai," students senior to you in your department, will give you an idea of the standard of English written by your peers.
2) Articles in leading international academic journals will provide you with examples of the highest standard of writing in English.
3) Conference proceedings, which usually contain much shorter versions of full papers presented at international conferences, will give you opportunities to quickly review the latest research.

Other good sources of high quality writing on academic topics can be found in the proceedings of inter-disciplinary conferences, the publications of inter-governmental bodies, the reports of non-governmental organizations, and in some cases, articles in quality newspapers and magazines.

There are three reasons why you should read as many English samples of good research writing as possible in the field you intend to research:

1) You need to find out what scholars and researchers in your field are writing about. One of the first steps in planning your own research project will be to select relevant research papers to study.
2) You need to learn how research in your field is written up.
3) You need to make decisions about what you can do to contribute to your field of study.

3. Membership in the research discourse community: Making connections and avoiding plagiarism

Originality in your own research is based on what you learn from reading the papers of other researchers. Your aim is to base your research on what other researchers in your field have already done. When you are reading about other people's research, you may get an idea for something that has never been done before and make a plan to do something completely new. However, most likely, at least in your first years as a researcher, you will think of a way to take a small, but valuable, step forward that will make a contribution to the work that other researchers have already done.

In any case, when you write up your research report, be very careful to give credit to your colleagues. This is the way you join the academic community. You become a member of the research discourse community in your field by making the links between your work and the work of others clear. In this way other researchers will recognize you as a colleague.

Quite obviously whenever you use words, charts, images and other information that you found in the research paper of another researcher or in any other source of information, you should state where you found that information. In addition, if you base your research concepts on someone else's ideas, you must state that in your paper. If you use any information, words, or ideas in your research that are not your own, you imply that it is your own intellectual property by not saying where you found it.

The use of someone else's research, without giving credit, is called "plagiarism." The Oxford Dictionary of English (Soanes & Stevenson, 2005, p. 1344), defines plagiarism as "the practice of taking someone else's work or ideas and passing them off as one's own."

There are four reasons that it is important to avoid plagiarism by making the connections between your work and the work of other people absolutely clear:

1) One of the most important conventions of writing research papers is giving credit to other researchers in the body of your paper as you refer to their work and at the end of your paper in a list of references. All researchers follow this practice.
2) You give your own work credibility by showing other researchers how your work fits into the research discourse community.
3) You can clarify for readers what is new about your research.
4) Accurate information about the basis of your research and your own contributions will help researchers who come after you add to your research.

4. Critical thinking: How to read like a researcher

Although "clarity" is rightly assumed to be a characteristic of academic writing in the descriptions of methodology and the presentations of findings, in research papers, especially in the discussions of findings and in the implications drawn in the conclusion, "vagueness" may be deliberately used. Partly, vagueness represents modesty in academic manners in which excessive claims may not only offend others in the community, but also be recklessly over confident when competing ideas may be presented at any time. Myers (1996) refers to strategic vagueness that allows results from different studies under somewhat different conditions to be compared, draws attention away from irrelevant parts of the findings, and encourages the assimilation of current and future developments in the field. In addition, a valuable function of vagueness is that it welcomes readers to do their own thinking and form independent evaluations.

Researchers engage in an analytical type of thinking, which is called *critical thinking*, while planning, conducting, and reporting on their research. Thus, you should also apply the same kind of thinking while reading research papers; indeed, a critical reading of research papers is, in itself, research. Critical thinking, as defined by Sumner (1940, pp. 632–633) is "the examination and test of propositions of any kind which are offered for acceptance, in order to find out whether they correspond to reality or not." Sumner claimed a central place for critical thinking in education and society because he said it is "our only guarantee against delusion, deception, superstition, and misapprehension of ourselves and our earthly circumstance."

How do you apply critical thinking? When you read research you hope to learn and remember information that is new to you. Learning the information in the research is not critical thinking; neither is remembering the information. Making decisions, forming judgments, and solving problems are not critical thinking either, unless you are thinking critically.

What does *thinking critically* mean? Paul, Binker, Jensen, and Kreklau (1990) list 35 skills in three categories: affective, micro-cognitive, and macro-cognitive strategies. For example, two affective strategies are developing intellectual humility and suspending judgment, and developing intellectual perseverance; cognitive strategy-macro abilities include refining generalizations and avoiding over-simplifications, and evaluating the credibility of sources of information; and examples of cognitive strategy-micro skills are distinguishing relevant from irrelevant facts, and exploring implications and consequences.

Willingham (2007, p. 11) explains how you can activate these strategies, abilities and skills. He identifies the characteristics of critical thinking as effectiveness, novelty, and self-direction:

> Critical thinking is effective in that it avoids common pitfalls, such as seeing only one side of an issue, discounting new evidence that disconfirms your ideas, reasoning from passion rather than logic, failing to support statements and so on. Critical thinking is novel in that you simply don't remember a solution or a situation that is similar enough to guide you. For example, solving a complex but familiar physics problem by applying a multi-step algorithm isn't critical thinking but devising a new algorithm is critical thinking. Critical thinking is self-directed in that the thinker must be calling the shots: We wouldn't give a student much credit for critical thinking if the teacher were prompting every step he took.

Critical thinking is a purposeful tool of analytical inquiry. On the basis of reflection on an analytical inquiry conducted while reading, (i.e., critically reading), you can make decisions about what the paper means, what you independently believe to be true and useful, and what you will do in response to the reading.

The views presented by the authors are based on the supporting evidence which they report. It is your responsibility to apply critical thinking to this evidence as you analyze, interpret, and evaluate research papers. Based on your evaluation of the implications of the research, you may make plans about what further research should be conducted or what other action should be taken.

In order that you may assess the value of a paper's findings, you should question the concepts the research is based on and the methods used to seek answers to the research. You may form your own views about the authors' criteria for the interpretation of the observations. Was the research conducted in a way which will allow the findings to be of use to other people in the field? If not, you may make personal judgments about the conclusions drawn from the research which differ from those of the authors.

A description of the critical reading involved in reading research papers could be summed up as follows:

1) the use of a set of thinking skills to analytically process information;
2) the generation of ideas which agree with, cast doubt upon, or add to, the concepts, methods, findings, and conclusions;
3) and the formation of personal beliefs.

5. What is the motivation for scholars to read critically?

1) It is a natural demonstration of constructive commitment to finding truth and usefulness.
2) Critical thinking reflects the norms and standards of scholarly inquiry which puts to the test the results of academic freedom. Academic freedom is defined by the University of Oxford Information and Communications Technology Strategic Plan(2007), on their website in this way:

> The most fundamental virtue, common to all universities, is academic freedom, which may be defined as the freedom to conduct research, teach, speak and publish, subject to the norms and standards of scholarly inquiry, without interference or penalty, wherever the search for truth and understanding may lead.

The posing of your own questions and the exercise of critical thinking skills while reading research is the application of scholarly inquiry. In this way, you open up a dialogue with an academic community which may help sustain academic freedom and intellectual integrity.

6. Conclusion

Is the capacity to think critically a natural part of your intelligence, or can "critical thinking" be taught and learned? In the *Nature and Nurture of Critical Thinking,* Halpern (2007, p. 10) claims, "There is a strong body of research to support the strong conclusion that specific instruction in thinking skills with diverse types of contexts (to encourage transfer across domains of knowledge) will enhance critical thinking skills." However, the core part of "instruction in thinking skills," to be truly critical thinking, should be self-instruction as you learn with other members of your community. In the next chapter, we will show that you can learn how to conduct an independent scholarly inquiry as you read research papers by asking questions that reflect critical thinking processes.

References

Halpern, D. (2007). The nature and nurture of critical thinking. In R. Sternberg, H. Roediger, & D. Halpern (Eds.), *Critical thinking in psychology* (pp. 1–14). Cambridge: Cambridge University Press.

Myers, G. (1996). Strategic vagueness in academic writing. In E. Ventola & A. Mauranen (Eds.), *Academic writing: Interculturral and textual issues* (pp. 3–18). Amsterdam: John Benjamins.

Paul, R., Binker., A., Jensen, K., & Kreklau, H. (1990). *Critical thinking handbook: A guide for remodeling lesson plans in language arts, social studies and science.* Rohnert Park, CA: Foundation for Critical Thinking.

Soanes, C., & Stevenson, A. (Eds.) (2005). *The Oxford Dictionary of English (2nd ed.).* Oxford: Oxford University Press.

Sumner, W. G. (1940). *Folkways: A study of the sociological importance of usages, manners, customs, mores, and morals.* New York: Ginn and Co.

University of Oxford (2007). Information and Communications Technology Strategic Plan, 2005–06 to 2009–10. Retrieved 24 September, 2009, from http://www.ict.ox.ac.uk/strategy/plan/plan.xml.ID=appF.

Willingham, D. (2007). Critical thinking: Why is it so hard to teach? *American Educator,* 8–19.

Learning Tasks

1) Conduct an Internet search on *critical thinking*. Be prepared to report on one interesting site.

2) Prepare a short essay on *critical thinking*.

3) Select three research papers. Based on the titles only, form questions that reflect *critical thinking*.

この章のまとめ

学術研究でもっとも重要なのは自ら考えることである．そのためには適切な方法を知っておく必要がある．critical thinking（批判的思考）は，これまであまり触れたことのない考え方だったかもしれない．しかし，先行研究，つまり学術論文を読み，自分のものとするためには，ぜひとも身につけておきたい考え方である．

用語説明

a) article
学術論文雑誌（journal）に掲載される論文のことを指す．多くの学術論文は査読と呼ばれる審査を経て掲載される．アカデミックライティングの目的の一つは，学術論文雑誌に掲載される論文を完成させる知識，技能を身につけることにある．

b) proceedings
各学会が開催する会議（conference）や大会（meeting）では，予稿集（proceedings）と呼ばれる研究発表の内容や概要をまとめたものが発行されることが多い．予稿集に掲載される原稿には，論文（full paper）と同じ質や量を持ったものから，要旨（abstract）程度のものまで千差万別であり，学会や大会の性質に依るところが大きい．

c) plagiarism
学術研究において，他人の研究成果を注釈なしに用いることを剽窃（盗用）といい，厳しく禁じられている．たとえ本人にその意志がなくても，厳しい処置が行われることもある．そのため，適切な引用方法を身につけておかなければならない．

Chapter 5
Critical Reading: An Application of Critical Thinking

Abstract

This chapter continues the discussion of critical thinking begun in Chapter 4 with a list of suggestions of questions for you to ask yourself while critically reading a research paper. To provide an overview of the questioning process, the suggestions are presented in the structural order of a research paper with questions for the title and abstract listed first and the conclusion last. Information is given about reading techniques for different reading purposes: "diving" for deep, thoughtful reading, "skimming" for rapid reading to get the gist of the paper, "scanning" to do key word searches, and "skipping" to re-read a paper to highlight the key parts for a later review of the paper. Advice is also given for note taking to record key information, and to sum up reflections on your critical thinking. To apply the critical thinking questions, the reading techniques, and the note taking methods, a 10-step critical reading strategy is proposed that recommends a particular order of reading: title, abstract, section headings, figures and tables, introduction, conclusion, and then, finally, the whole paper from the beginning to the end. The chapter concludes with a brief consideration of a goal close to the hearts of many students, the hope of becoming a bilingual researcher.

♦ Keywords

Bilingual researcher, Critical reading questions, Research paper reading strategies, Reading techniques

この章のねらい

前章では学術研究での考え方，critical thinking について紹介した．この章ではこの考え方をより実践的な方法で深めていく．学術論文の読み方の具体的な手順を示していくので，この章だけをただ読むのではなく，興味のある学術論文を手に入れて，論文と平行しながら読み進めてほしい．

1. Introduction

This chapter has several lists of suggestions about reading research papers. We do not expect you to accept our advice, uncritically, as the best suggestions for you. We expect you to use our advice as starting points for your own critical thinking about how to read articles. You should experiment with various reading approaches, assess the effectiveness of your trial-and-error approach, and make on-going adjustments to your own critical reading techniques as you learn to read by reading.

Why are we paying so much attention to reading in this writing book? Greenhalgh defines research in her book, *How to read a paper: The basics of evidence-based medicine* as "focused, systematic inquiry aimed at generating new knowledge" (2006, p. 1). The inquiry is a partnership of those who conduct the research and those who read it. The research reports are the means of communication. Although Greenhalgh's (2006) advice is intended for medical students and practitioners, its common sense is widely applicable. She describes reading as a critical observation technique that is fundamental to research in any field.

Reading other researchers' reports allows you access to their critical thinking processes and thus, provides you with opportunities to participate in the generation of new knowledge by independently assessing the reports and determining how it may be applied to your own work. This chapter about how to read research papers is also about learning how to conduct and write up your own research.

2. Critical reading

2.1 Critical reading: What questions do you ask when you apply "critical thinking" to reading research?

It is important to keep in mind that learning to read research reports will be a life-long and satisfying task for many of you. You will have time to gradually develop sophisticated academic reading skills over many years. Nonetheless, it is important to get off to a good start. To read like a researcher, it is important to pose your own research questions as you read.

There is a great deal of easily accessible on-line advice in English provided by universities for their students on how to ask questions as you read a research paper. To find this advice, conduct an Internet search using the following key words: "how to read a research paper" ("article," "report," or "study"), "how to read and evaluate a research article," "critical reading strategies," and "critical reading questions."

The suggestions on the great number of advice sites naturally have a great deal in common. Academic writing guides for students usually claim that the basic principles of research writing apply to the full range of broadly related branches of study (see Craswell, 2005; Gustavii, 2003; Turabian, 2007). The same is likely true for the basic principles of reading research writing. You may confirm this proposition by surveying websites on reading research. We recommend the following seven websites:

1) Harvard College Library website. Look for the section called Interrogating Texts: 6 Reading Habits to Develop in Your First Year at Harvard:
   http://hcl.harvard.edu/research/guides/lamont_handouts/interrogatingtexts.html
   Most universities have on-line Student Counseling Services and Library pages with advice on academic reading, and writing skills. Many are quite similar and you can benefit by visiting only a few of the thousands of sites. Visit the sites of universities that you are interested in.
2) The University of British Columbia Library website has information from the Writers Center with useful links to sites of other universities: http://toby.library.ubc.ca/webpage/webpage.cfm?id=511
3) The website of the Lewy Body Dementia Association has a guide for people who need help in reading research papers in fields new to them. Look for the article entitled, Increasing Knowledge: How To Read a Research Paper:
   http://www.lbda.org/feature/2192/increasing-knowledge-and-how-to-read-a-research-paper.htm
4) The Rice University "Connexions" website has a useful article called How to Read a Scientific Article:
   http://cnx.org/content/m15912/latest/
5) How to Read an Engineering Research Paper:
   http://cseweb.ucsd.edu/~wgg/CSE210/howtoread.html

6) How to Read a Legal Opinion: A Guide for New Law Students:
http://volokh.com/files/howtoread2007version.pdf
7) The Heal website has a very clear guide on reading medical research intended for non-medical people:
http://healtoronto.com/howto.html
The author of this guide, Trisha Greenhalgh, has a series of ten articles on reading medical research papers for medical students and practitioners with summaries of her key points published online by the *British Medical Journal*. This summary provides useful advice for any type of scientific paper. In addition, her book, *How to read a paper: The basics of evidence-based medicine* (Greenhalgh, 2006), is available in a Japanese translation.

2.2 A list of questions for critical reading

We have created a list of suggestions for questions to ask while reading based on the commonalities of conventional advice (see the websites listed above) and on our understanding of Japanese university students. In another section of this chapter we will suggest that you do not first read a research paper straight through from the beginning to the end. However, for the time being we will present our first suggestions in an order which will give you an easy-to-understand overview. The following 10-point list contains examples of critical reading questions that might be asked as you read through a research paper from the title to the list of references that follow the conclusion.

1) What does the *title* say about the general theme and the specific focus of the paper? What do you want to learn from this paper? What questions do you have about it?
2) What information does the *abstract* provide? What does it say about the purposes, the research questions, the findings and the conclusion? What questions do you have about the information in the abstract and what else, in addition to this information, do you want to find in the paper? Is the paper going to investigate a controversy? Is it going to demonstrate a new technique? Is it going to introduce a new field of study?
3) How do the *introduction* and the *literature review* explain how the research fits into its field? Do you agree with the author's justification, the rationale, for the research? Why is this research important?

4) Is a *hypothesis* clearly stated? Will the research questions be a reasonable test of the hypothesis? Can you foresee any challenges in answering these questions?
5) Do you have any questions about the *methods*? If people were studied, do these people usefully represent the intended broader group of people? Were the measurements the best way to find answers to the research questions?
6) What are the most important *findings*? Were they expected? Based on the evidence presented in the paper, could you make your own analysis and come up with your own answers to the research questions? Would your analysis and your answers be similar to those of the author? Did you notice any interesting points in the findings that were not mentioned in the discussion? Do you have other ways of explaining the findings?
7) Would you have come to the same *conclusions*? Has the researcher been cautious and based the conclusions only upon the evidence? Are there additional research questions about other relevant factors that should have been considered?
8) What was the main *contribution* of the research project?
9) What research do you think could be done next? Would you do research yourself in this area?
10) Are there any papers listed in the *references* section that you think you may need to read in future for your own study?

We recommend that you use our suggestions as a starting point and come up with your own ideas which you can discuss with your classmates and experiment with as you read research reports. Please get some first-language baseline data; i.e., how do you effectively and efficiently read research articles in Japanese? Make comparisons between your baseline data and the advice for reading in English to find similarities and differences. Make an advice list that suits Japanese university students in general and you in particular.

3. Reading techniques: Diving, skimming, scanning, skipping

A variety of research initiatives that have explored various types of reading strategies non-native English speaking university students use in reading English seem to agree that a questioning approach; i.e., *critical thinking,* is effective when it leads to a sophisticated understanding of the content of a text and how the text is related to other aspects of study. Marton and Saljo (1997) claim that this type of "deep" approach to reading often reflects intrinsic motivation. The contrasting "surface" approach may be quite common (Chalmers & Fuller, 1995); possibly when extrinsically motivated students are satisfied with just getting through their reading assignments without a rigorous application of effective reading techniques (Prosser & Trigwell, 1999). Metacognitive reading strategies, or the ability to think about thinking (O'Malley & Chamot, 1990), may be the single distinguishing feature of successful academic reading. Reading strategies are implemented by reading techniques; thus, you must develop a repertoire of techniques that allow you to put your critical reading strategies into action. The Academic Skills Unit on the University of Melbourne's Academic Enrichment homepage has a reading strategies page (http://www.services.unimelb.edu.au/asu/reading/strategies/index.html) which describes three widely-used reading techniques: scanning, skimming and SQ3R: surveying, questioning, reading, reciting, and reviewing. We suggest that you experiment with a revised set of four techniques: diving, skimming, scanning, and skipping.

1) When you first read the *title* and the *abstract,* the *introduction* and the *conclusion* section of the paper, take all the time you need to dive into the paper and give a deep reading to these sections so that your understanding is as deep as possible at this stage. Do not stay on the surface by reading slowly word by word. Read concept by concept as quickly as you can. When you are a veteran researcher, your broad background knowledge will help you get a good general understanding of the whole paper from a *diving* reading of just these four parts of a paper, plus the figures and tables in the results section.
2) Use a reading technique called *skimming* to get a quick overview of the whole paper. When you skim a paper, you should read about three times faster than a diving reading. Do not focus on details. Try to get the main ideas and keep going. Skimming is a useful reading technique for the first fast reading of the whole research paper.
3) When you want to look for important words from the *title,* the *abstract,* or the *keywords list* on the first page of the paper, use a reading technique

called *scanning* to quickly search for those words in the other sections of the paper. Scanning may be twice as fast as skimming. When you locate those words, you may find that the sections of the paper around the key words are important and should be highlighted. Scanning is useful when you want to review the paper quickly by identifying the most important parts and also when you want to review a certain concept in a paper.

4) If you have identified the paper as very important to your own study, you may want to use the deep reading technique for most of the paper. However, if you are reading many papers as a general review of the literature, *skipping* is a technique that allows you to read more quickly, as you do when skimming, but also lets you pause and slow down for a deep reading when you find something very important or very difficult to understand.

4. Keeping records: Critical thinking and note-taking skills

Why should you take notes while reading papers? The title, author, and location of the paper is the way you will find the paper again when you need it. *Note taking* is a very good way to identify the main points of the research because your notes need to be brief but useful. It is the best way to remember months later what the research was about. It is a first step in writing your own paper. You can connect the notes you have made from different sources in an order that will become the story line of your paper. The story line is a list of a few key words that you can write in a flow chart as you do the initial planning of your own research paper. The following suggestions on note taking may be useful:

1) If you plan to keep a copy of the paper on file, highlight the key parts of the article. The highlighting will serve as a form of notes and help you review the paper quickly later.
2) Write the identification data for the paper (i.e., author, title, publishing information) in the same style you will use when you write the research paper (e.g., the American Psychological Association (APA) style–see the references–has been used in this book).
3) Keep your notes in two languages for all your research. Use both languages

to note vocabulary and concepts that are new to you. Make English notes to learn the language of your research field.
4) It is best to use a computer software file to save, and backup, all of your notes. The most efficient way to write and revise a complex set of information is not with pencil and paper.
5) When you make your notes it is not necessary to write complete sentences. Do not worry too much about grammar and spelling at the note-taking stage. It is a good idea to use abbreviations wherever possible.
6) Be as brief as possible but you need to include all of the main points and each main point's supporting points. Organize these points in a logical order.
7) Do not copy sections of the paper you are reading but write a summary in your own words. Only copy if you need to directly quote from the paper and then make a careful note of the page number.

Most likely, you will develop your own unique note-taking system. Whatever system you use, make sure that your filing system will continue working as you add notes year by year. Most importantly, make your notes detailed enough so that you can understand them when you read them again months later.

5. Learning academic vocabulary

One of the best reasons to read academic papers is to improve your vocabulary in the specific areas of study that you are personally interested in. You will meet many words you are not familiar with, especially at first.
The following list of general suggestions may be useful:

1) Do not read a paper word by word, line by line, highlighting every word and phrase you don't understand. Be satisfied with understanding the main points. Look up only the words you feel are important to the paper and words that are special to the field.
2) An ordinary dictionary may not be good enough. Some words have a special academic meaning. For example *significant* in English for general purposes means personally evaluated as important; however, it has a special academic sense that is used when the difference between groups

is large enough to be statistically reliable. Make sure you find a definition of words in the ways scholars and researchers use them. That means the definition will be very precise and used in a limited way. Use a dictionary made for the field that the paper is in. For example, you may need to use a medical dictionary to find the meaning of *blot* as it is used in medical research. It can refer to a procedure which uses *Southern blot analysis* to test the ability of a nucleic acid probe from one species to hybridize with the DNA fragment of another species. An ordinary dictionary may define *blot* as a spot or a stain that spoils something.

3) Experiment with ways to learn the new words. Find out what works best for you.

6. A 10-step strategy for critically reading English research papers

You may find that reading a research paper from the beginning to the end is not the best way for you to understand the paper.

1) Read the *title* with the "diving" reading technique. Begin making a vocabulary list. The title should tell you exactly what the paper is about. If the title is in two parts separated by a colon, the first part will likely be the broad theme and the second part will describe the focus of the research. Begin making critical thinking notes as you ask yourself questions.

2) Use the "diving" technique again to read the *abstract*. Add words to your vocabulary list. Following the abstract on some papers is a *keywords list* of 5 or 6 words which are related to the central concepts of the paper. Some of these key words may be found in the title and the abstract. Use the "scanning" reading technique to look for the key words in the paper.

3) Read the *headings* of each section of the paper. If the headings are simply an indication of the function of the section; e.g., Introduction, read the first paragraph of the section to get an idea of the content of the section. In some cases, a heading may tell you more about the purpose of the section; e.g., Introduction: identifying key weaknesses of the current system. This is a good time to look at the *figures* and the *tables* because they likely sum up essential messages of their section of the paper. Figures

and tables will likely be found in the results section.
4) Read the *introduction* and the *conclusion* with the "diving" technique. These two sections are the book ends of the paper that hold the content in order just as book ends keep books together in a desired order.
5) When you have a general idea of the content you will start to read the whole paper. Use the "skimming" reading technique to read fairly quickly. The purpose is to get an overview of the whole paper. Read the whole paper again with the "skipping" technique. During this second reading based on your skimming reading, you can make choices about where to slow your reading down for the parts you feel are most important.
6) Read the *discussion* section of the paper carefully with the "diving" reading technique because it contains the conclusions that the author would like to draw from the data. This is usually where the author reflects on the work and its meaning in relation to other findings and to the field in general.
7) Skim through the list of *references*. You may find the next paper you want to read in the list. Notice how the references are written. When you write your own paper, you will be required to use one of the common systems for writing a references list.
8) Read the critical thinking notes you made while reading. Eliminate the unnecessary.
9) Add new thoughts and new questions you have at this stage to your notes.
10) Review your vocabulary list. Make a plan for regular reviews.

7. Becoming a bilingual researcher: A two-language reading plan

If you read in your field in English, you will have access to a global research library. If you write about your academic work in English, you can share your ideas with international academic communities. If you can do your research reading in Japanese and English and your writing in two languages as well, you will truly be a bilingual researcher with a role to play on the Japanese and the international academic stages.

Thus, it seems reasonable to make a two-language research reading plan.

How much time do you actually have to read in a week, in one semester, and in the vacation time? Set realistic targets. Naturally, the volume of your reading in Japanese will be the greatest. Indeed, your reading in Japanese should come first because it will support your reading in English as you gradually come to understand more about the foundations of, and the progress of, developments in your field. It is also important to learn about the structure, style, and vocabulary used in research writing in Japanese to be able to make useful comparisons with English.

How about starting your two-language reading plan by setting a five to one Japanese/English ratio? For every five academic articles you read in Japanese, try to read one in English. Then, adjust the ratio to fit in with your own schedule but continue to try to read research in both languages regularly.

Reading research papers can be compared to listening to lectures and to talking to your teachers. The authors of the papers you read become, in a very real sense, your teachers. Someday if you become an active scholar, you will be a colleague of the authors of the papers you have read, by learning to conduct, and write about, your own research.

8. Conclusion

The purpose of reading research reports in English is to make you a better researcher yourself by engaging in critical thinking as you read so that you are able to accomplish three important tasks: add to your base of knowledge of what is happening in your field, decide what sort of research you want to do yourself, and learn how other researchers write their reports. The reports you read will serve as models for your own writing but it is essential to learn by doing. In other words, provide your own models of writing by starting to write as soon as possible and then, by writing as often as possible. Revise your own writing, again and again, as you continue to read. As you use Part II of this book, try to become good at writing by first becoming good at rewriting.

References

American Psychological Association. (2006). *Publication manual of the American Psychological Association. (6th ed.)*. Washington: American Psychological Association.

Chalmers, D., & Fuller, R. (1995). *Teaching for learning at university: Theory and practice*. Perth: Edith Cowan University.

Craswell, G. (2005). *Writing for academic success: A postgraduate guide*. London: Sage Publications Ltd.

Greenhalgh, T. (2006). *How to read a paper: The basics of evidence-based medicine*. Oxford: Blackwell Publishing Ltd.

Gustavii, B. (2003). *How to write and illustrate a scientific paper*. Cambridge: Cambridge University Press.

Marton, F., & Saljo, R. (1997). Approaches to learning. In F. Marton, D. Hounsell, & N. J. Entwistle (Eds.), *The experience of learning: Implications for teaching and studying in higher education* (2nd ed.) (pp. 39–58). Edinburgh: Scottish Academic Press.

O'Malley, J., & Chamot, A. (1990). *Learning strategies in second language acquisition*. Cambridge: Cambridge University Press.

Prosser, M., & Trigwell, K. (1999). *Understanding learning and teaching: The experience in higher education*. Malabar: Open University Press.

Turabian, K. (2007). *A manual for writers of research papers, theses, and dissertations: Chicago style for students and researchers*. Chicago: University of Chicago Press.

Learning Tasks

1) Prepare a list of Japanese and English research journals in your field.

2) Make a list of academic conferences–single disciplinary and inter-disciplinary in Japan and overseas.

3) Select a research paper and try the 10-step strategy suggested in this chapter.

この章のまとめ

アカデミックライティングには，学術論文を読むという行為が欠かせない．また，学術論文はただ読むのではなく，一定の方法でもって読み進めていかなければ意味がない．ここで学んだ考え方，読み方は今後の研究生活の中で常に意識しておいてほしい．

用語説明

a) rationale
研究を行うにあたっては，なぜその研究を行うのかという理由を論理的に組み立てなければならない．研究の根拠となる理論的な裏付けのことをrationaleという．rationaleを明確にするには，先行研究の十分な分析と検討が必要になる．

b) semester
大学などにおける学期のことを指す．現在，日本では，多くの大学が前期・後期の二学期制を採用しており，それぞれの学期のことを指してセメスター（semester）と呼ぶことが多い．

Part II

Writing an Academic Paper

Introduction to Part II

　パートIIでは，パートIで学んだアカデミックライティングの考え方を実践する．現在，実際に学術論文を生産している研究者も，最初から論文を書けたわけではない．どのように学術論文を組み立てていくのか，特にパートIで学んだ考え方をどのように活かしていくのか，今いる地点から少しずつ高いレベルを目指して読み進めていこう．学術論文の作成は，センスや才能がなければできないというものではなく，適切な手順と方法を知っているか，それらに熟練しているかどうかこそが重要である．

　まずは，自分の考えを元に論文の形となるものを作っていくところから始める．いきなり全体を仕上げようとするのではなく，少しずつ積み上げていけばよい．しかし，どのように積み上げればよいのだろうか．そのためには必要な手順を知っておかなければならない．必要なのは全体の構造とそれらを支える個々の構造である．

　6章では，アウトラインから全体を書き上げる方法を学ぶ．7章では，議論を深め，サポートするための論文の探し方や読み方を学ぶ．8章，9章ではabstractとintroductionという論文の一部の執筆を練習する．10章が論文本体の執筆となるが，ここでは主に論文の文章の構造について学ぶことになる．11章と12章は論文の仕上げについての章であり，11章で論文のまとめ方と12章で適切な引用方法とそれらの提示方法を学ぶ．パートIIはただ読むだけではなく，実際に手を動かすことが重要である．自分なりの英語論文を作り上げていってほしい．

Chapter 6

Writing the Outline and the First Draft

この章のねらい
この章では，書き始めるまでの準備を実践する．アカデミックライティングでは，いきなり文章を書き始めることはしない．書き始める前に十分な準備を行わなければならない．書き始めるにあたって，特に重要となるのはアイデアである．アイデアをどのようにして膨らませ，「書く」レベルまで発展させていくのか．その方法を順番に見ていこう．

Writing is a *process*. What does that mean? Basically, it means that a writer works through a number of steps to produce a piece of writing. In this chapter, you will work through these steps: getting ideas to write about; developing your ideas; developing a research plan; planning an academic paper; revising your plan; and, writing a first draft.

1. Developing your learning

Learning Task 1

Think about these questions and write your answers. Then, work with a partner and ask him/her each of the questions. Discuss your answers.

a. Do you like to write?
b. What kind of academic writing have you done so far?
c. When you are given a writing assignment, what do you normally do first?
d. What subjects and topics are you most interested in?
e. How do you get ideas for writing topics?

2. Developing ideas for writing assignments

Learning Task 2

How many books, newspapers and magazines do you normally read each week? Ask classmates sitting near you.

As you know from Part I of this book good writing starts with quality reading. This is true in at least two ways. First, writers need models of what is appropriate and what is good style. Second, good writing needs interesting and robust ideas. As a university student, you must read regularly and widely. You should also try to discuss what you are reading with peers.

2.1 Getting ideas

Learning Task 3

Work in a group of 2–4 students and discuss responses for Question 1–e in Section 1 above. Fill in the graphic below with information from your discussion.

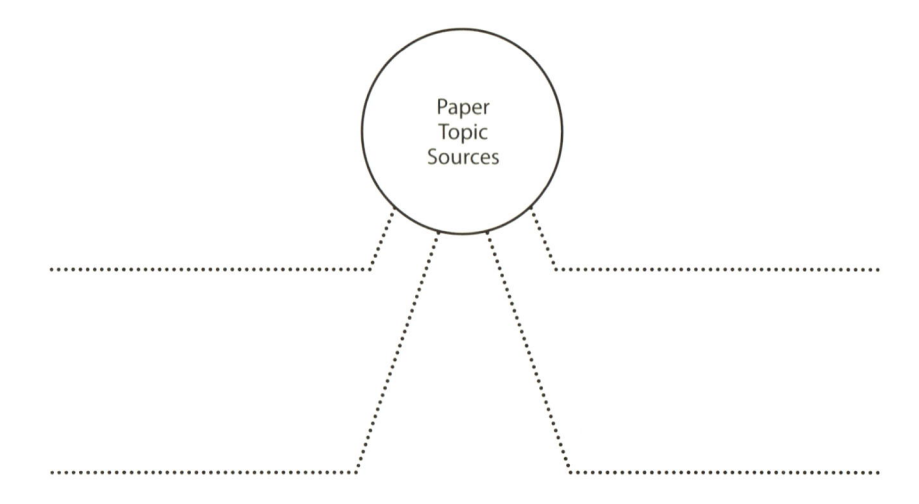

Paper
Topic
Sources

2.2 Listing ideas

Discovering, linking, and organizing ideas before writing is an essential step to good, clear academic writing. Many people list their ideas prior to beginning writing. Begin by thinking about a topic in general terms (e.g., whales) and list what you know about it. This will help you develop and find a focus for your paper topic.

Whales

- cetology (study of whales & dolphins)
- social mammals
- songs (language/intelligence?)
- school lunches (Japan)
- IWC (International Whaling Commission)
- "scientific" whaling (Japan)
- Greenpeace arrests (Japan)
- populations growing

2.3 Focusing a topic

An outline is basically a sketch of your paper. Once you have a general topic idea you need to focus it. Why is this important? The reason is to make your writing clear. It is not possible to write a good paper if you write too broadly on a topic, but writers often find it difficult to narrow, or limit, a topic. Finding a topic focus that is limited enough can take time as you think through (and read more about) a given subject.

One way to approach finding a topic focus is think about topics in general and specific terms. Consider the general topic of whales, for example. If you try to write a paper on whales in general, it will obviously be too broad. A good topic would be much more focused. For example,

whales
whales → scientific whaling
whales → scientific whaling → international protest
whales → scientific whaling → international protest → Sea Shepherd

Paper topic: Is the Sea Shepherd's protest activity legitimate?

Note that this topic is formulated as a question. Academic writing is related to research and research is about asking and investigating questions. We can call such questions *research questions*. The topic for a paper together with the research question(s) might change as you research and think more deeply. After all, writing is thinking.

Learning Task 4

Think of ways to focus these general topics:
a) Education
b) Poverty
c) Cloning

Learning Task 5

Compare your focused topics with those of your classmates. Which topics do you think are the clearest and most interesting?

2.4 Paper planning steps

What are the steps involved in planning an academic paper? How would you order the steps? Some suggestions are listed in the box below. Can you think of more?

Learning Task 6

Add more steps and list them in the order that you would use to **plan** your paper. Compare your ideas with those of classmates.

| read | supporting details | main ideas | title |

2.5 Define your audience

As you begin to plan your research paper, you should consider an academic audience (see Chapter 1). Who will be reading your research paper (i.e., teachers, peers, experts, generalists)? Academic writing is done for members of an academic discourse community. It is important to remember that people in the academic community do not communicate in writing by simply reporting information. They write with the purpose of addressing a research question or problem, and developing an argument or providing information related to the argument in order to inspire other members of the academic discourse community to think and ask questions. Therefore, if you are assigned to write a paper for a university class, avoid simply writing about your personal opinions, beliefs, feelings, and experiences—unless your professor gives you permission to do this. Opinions need to be *informed,* and that means you need to support your opinions with evidence.

3. Research plan

Learning Task 7

Use the guidance in Sections 2.2 and 2.3 of this chapter to determine a topic you would like to study. What are your research questions? How will you research the paper topic? Outline a research plan. If you do not have a topic in mind, you can refer to the topic of climate change.

Topic:

Audience:

What I want to know about the topic: (appropriate for my audience?)

Research questions:

Information search (type of sources; What sources do you currently know?)

Completion dates: (schedule your writing)

Draft 1 _____

Draft 2 _____

Final draft _____

4. Practice exercises

The practice exercises below ask you to separately examine the steps involved in writing an English for General Academic Purposes (EGAP) paper. Whenever you begin a paper outline, you should carefully consider each of these features. All of the examples in this section find their source in Kyoto University first-year student papers.

4.1 Title

For EGAP papers, titles should be short, descriptive, but at the same time, attention-grabbing.

Learning Task 8

Below, four example titles are listed. Which titles do you think are the clearest? Can you think of another possible title for this topic?

Paper Topic: Climate change
  Title 1: Paper
  Title 2: Earth's Climate
  Title 3: Environmental Crossroads
  Title 4: Global Warming

  Your Idea: _____

Learning Task 9

> Which title or titles do you think are the most descriptive for this topic? Explain to a classmate.

A Note on Titles

It is useful to have a *working title* as you start writing an academic paper. This means that your final title could be different. In fact, the title is the last thing that many writers choose to write. Your title should reflect the content of your paper, the main point in your thesis statement, and the type of finding (i.e., surprising, unusual, predictable, uncertain, preliminary and so forth).

4.2 Thesis statement

Writing a thesis statement for a paper is a very useful practice for at least two reasons.

a. If you cannot state your ideas in one or two sentences, then the topic may not be focused.
b. Thesis statements are summaries of your topic focus and help you organize and develop your argument.

Good thesis statements:
- are clear and express one main idea;
- are specific to the assignment requirements; and,
- assert your conclusions about a subject.

4.2.1 Steps for generating a thesis statement

Step 1: Brainstorm the topic
You might start out with a very general topic idea like this:

Climate change

But since this statement is very general, it is not a thesis statement. Because it is so general, readers of your paper would not have a clear idea of what you want to say about changes of the Earth's climate.

Step 2: Narrow the topic

After some thought you might find that climate change is not the most accurate term and, as you read more, you might decide to link this topic to the most comprehensive treaty on climate to date. Therefore, you revise your thesis statement like this:

Climate destruction and the Kyoto Protocol

This fragment focuses the topic of the research paper on the Kyoto Protocol to the United Nations Framework Convention on Climate Change, but the statement is still not clear. In addition, since your conclusion remains unclear it is not yet a thesis statement.

Step 3: Clarify your stance

After reflecting on the topic again, you decide that what you really want to focus on is the local area (i.e., Kansai region) response to the climate issue, specifically the targets of the Kyoto Protocol. Your revised thesis statement looks like this:

Local action supporting the Kyoto Protocol targets

This is a specific statement, but it is not yet a thesis statement as it needs more clearly outlined support.

Step 4: Make a specific assertion based on clearly stated support

You revise your statement one last time to look like this:

The situation with climate change is becoming critical for human civilization. In this paper, I will first argue that humans are causing climate destruction and that human activity must be checked. I will then provide a basic outline of the Kyoto Protocol of 1997 and describe how institutions in the Kansai region of Japan are taking action in support of the protocol.

This thesis statement answers the question, "How significant is climate change and how is it being addressed?" It is useful to organize your paper around research questions.

4.3 Main ideas & supporting details

As with a title, you will surely begin writing your paper with a *working thesis statement* that will develop as you write and think through your ideas. Writing helps people to think about their ideas carefully and as you write you will often find that your ideas change. Writing is a process, so writers do not wait for the perfect plan to emerge before they start writing. You write from your current level of understanding. Below is a draft plan of main ideas and supporting details related to the topic climate change. There are four main points and under each main point is listed between one and three supporting details.

Current situation
- a. background description
- b. human impact
- c. most descriptive term & definition—climate destruction

Kyoto Protocol
- a. main goals

Local actions
- a. describe 1–2 actions by Kansai governments/businesses
- b. think of what else could be done

How serious is climate change?
- a. Are people doing enough?

4.4 Headings & subheadings

Why should you put headings and subheadings into your paper? The simple answer is that headings help readers to understand your writing. Academic papers always include section headings for clarity. Study the keywords and ideas in the main sections of your paper to create headings.

Learning Task 10

For the main ideas described above, possible headings could be those in the box below. Do you prefer the headings in Column A or the ones in column B? Why?

A-headings	B-headings
Current Situation	**Human Impact on Earth's Climate**
Kyoto Protocol	**The Kyoto Protocol**
Local Actions	**Kansai Activity Supporting the**
Are People Doing Enough?	**Kyoto Protocol**
	Conclusion

4.5 Rhetorical modes of organization

For all sections of your academic paper (i.e., introduction, body, and conclusion), there are several common ways to organize information into particular patterns. These are sometimes called *rhetorical functions, rhetorical modes,* or *patterns of organization*. In this book, we refer to them as rhetorical modes. Some of the common rhetorical modes used in academic writing are:

Narration: to tell a story.
Description: to represent something with words.
Exemplification: to provide examples.
Cause and effect: to report research that suggests causal relationships.
Problem/Solution: to identify a problem and possible solutions.
Extended Definition/Classification: to define a technical term and/or place the term into a context through classification.
Comparison/Contrast: to compare is to consider similarities; to contrast is to consider differences.
Argumentation: to take a position on an issue or problem that is based on evidence and logic.

(See Chapter 10 for detailed information about rhetorical modes.)

4.6 Example of a paper outline

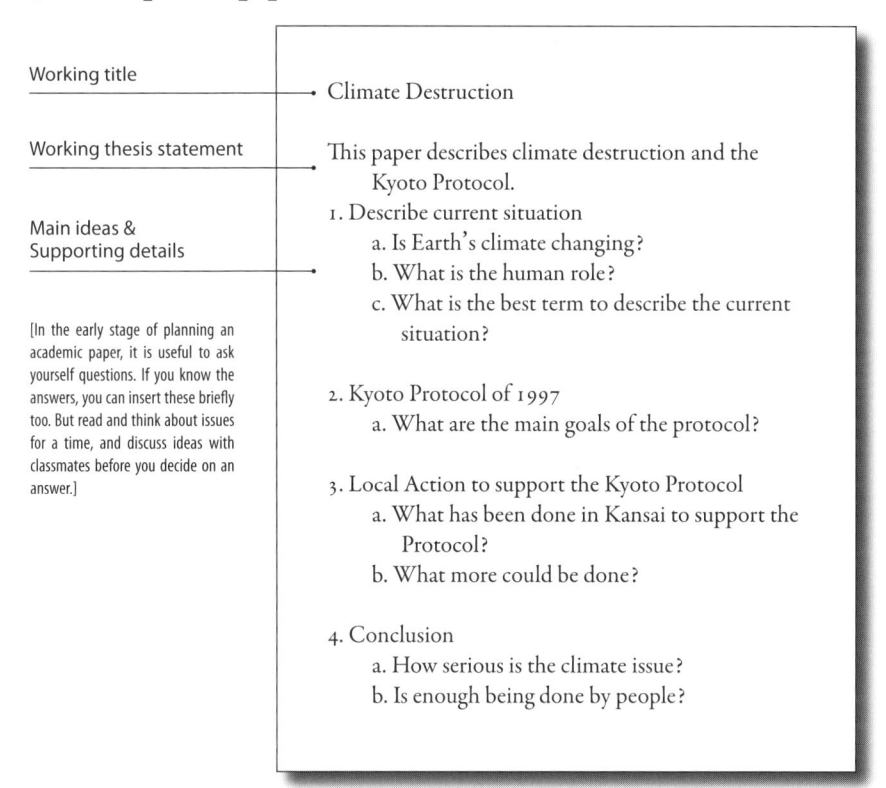

Working title

→ Climate Destruction

Working thesis statement

This paper describes climate destruction and the Kyoto Protocol.

Main ideas & Supporting details

1. Describe current situation
   a. Is Earth's climate changing?
   b. What is the human role?
   c. What is the best term to describe the current situation?

[In the early stage of planning an academic paper, it is useful to ask yourself questions. If you know the answers, you can insert these briefly too. But read and think about issues for a time, and discuss ideas with classmates before you decide on an answer.]

2. Kyoto Protocol of 1997
   a. What are the main goals of the protocol?

3. Local Action to support the Kyoto Protocol
   a. What has been done in Kansai to support the Protocol?
   b. What more could be done?

4. Conclusion
   a. How serious is the climate issue?
   b. Is enough being done by people?

5. Moving from outline to draft one

Writing is a mysterious process. Until we finish writing, the actual topic focus can often remain unclear. And, of course, reading is a kind of intellectual journey that cannot be separated from writing. As we start reading something, we are not exactly sure where the writer will take us. Therefore, when planning your writing it helps to think of your paper outline like a map. As a writer, you are like a tour guide introducing a new place (new ideas) to readers. Try to make a clear plan for your paper because in academic writing, clarity is highly valued. Talk about your plan with classmates and your teacher. You may understand your outline (map), but it might not be so clear to other people. There could be gaps in your plan.

5.1 Create an outline

Learning Task 11

Use the information in Section 4 (Practice Exercises) of this chapter and create an outline for your paper.

5.2 Discuss your outline

Learning Task 12

Talk to at least two classmates. Tell them about your paper plan by describing your outline.

5.3 Revise your outline

Learning Task 13

Consider the questions below carefully and decide how you will revise the outline for your academic paper.

- What did you learn from your classmates?
- Did your classmates have any problems understanding your ideas? If so, what?
- Did you get any new ideas from your classmates?
- How will you revise your outline?

Notes:

5.4 Sample paper draft

Once you are satisfied with your outline you are ready to start writing. Here is a partial first draft of a paper as an example. Please note how it is organized.

Working title (name, student number, date, etc.)	The Climate Crisis
Heading	**Defining the Issue**
Introduction • provide general topic background • working thesis statement	Today the earth is facing great difficulties related to food, population and the environment. People are especially concerned with abnormal weather because it concerns the lives of people all over the world. My position is that the situation with regard to climate change is becoming critical for human civilization. In this paper, I will argue that climate destruction is largely anthropocentric and must be checked. I will then provide a basic outline of the Kyoto Protocol of 1997 and describe how institutions in the Kansai region of Japan are taking action in support of the protocol.
• define key terms	I believe that the best term to describe the current situation is 'climate destruction' because …
Body (heading)	**The Kyoto Protocol**
Outline the status quo • cite sources for key information	The 1997 Kyoto Protocol to the United Nations Framework Convention on Climate Change is the only international agreement on global warming (Kyoto Protocol, 1997). The Protocol has a goal to reduce greenhouse gases "by at least 5 percent below 1990 levels" in the period 2008 to 2012. Each nation is assigned specific numerical targets …
Heading	**Local Actions**
	Japan must reduce greenhouse gas emissions by 6% of 1990 levels between 2008 and 2012, but these

[annotation: Link theoretical and practical issues whenever possible]

levels are actually rising. Therefore, in Kansai many schools and offices are trying to realize the goal of the Kyoto Protocol. 'Eco bags' are now very popular in Kansai and there is a 'my bag' boom (Nakano, 2008). For example, the stores at Kyoto University no longer offer customers plastic bags for goods.

In addition, Kyoto City began to …

[annotation: Suggest alternatives]

These efforts are good, but I believe people can do more. I know from talking to foreign visitors that many of them are disappointed in the traffic situation in Kyoto. Since the Kyoto Protocol was negotiated here, people believe that Kyoto should be a model for the world. Therefore, I encourage Kyoto and Kansai to become 'green cities.' For example, some roads should be closed to traffic on national holidays and Sundays to encourage people to walk and bicycle. Also, Kyoto University has many bicycles and students ride on sidewalks. This is dangerous for pedestrians but they do so because there are no designated bike pathways in the city. Kyoto should create a network of bicycle pathways immediately …

Conclusion

[annotation: Conclusion (heading); reflect on your main points; assess the situation; restate your main idea]

Many scientists say that the present situation is very serious. They claim that if we do not change climate destruction will continue as the surface temperature will rise from 4 to 6 °C (Flannery, 2006). This means that humans need to do more to change the situation …

References

[annotation: References (heading); list all of the sources you researched for the paper]

See Chapter 12 for examples of how to use APA citation style.

[annotation: Page numbers (footer)]

1

5.5 Write a first draft

Learning Task 14

Type your first draft according to these specifications. You want your work to look professional. Learn how to use your word processing software program. As you work through the following chapters, you will revise your first draft into a finished product.

Leave margins of 2 centimeters top, bottom, left, and right.

Title

Center your title and use 14-point font

Name: Date:
Student number:
Day/Period

Type your name and student number as well as the date and the day/period of the class

Remember to use headings.

Heading 1

When you begin typing, don't forget to indent!

Double-space the text!

Start typing your paper after indenting 5 spaces (2 tabs). You can set the tabs on the 'first line indent'. Remember never to touch the 'return' (enter) key until you want to begin a new paragraph.

Indent (2 tabs) at the start of each new paragraph.

Use the header/footer function and insert a page number

1

6. Developing your learning

In the first part of this chapter you answered the following question:

> When you are given a writing assignment, what do you normally do first?
>
> Has your response to this question changed? Why or why not?

この章のまとめ

ドラフトを書くまでの道のりはどうだっただろうか．アイデアを出すところから始めて，トピックとタイトルを決め，満足のいくアウトラインを作ることができただろうか．途中で鍵となるのは，thesis statements，主題文という考えである．アイデアだけでは漠然としているため，議論の焦点をはっきりとさせ，書き始めるまでに十分なレベルに狭めていかなければならない．主題文によってアイデアの形がはっきりすれば，アウトラインの組み立てもスムーズに行えるようになる．主題文の重要性が理解できるまで，繰り返し練習を行ってみるとよいだろう．

Chapter 7 Researching an Academic Paper

> **この章のねらい**
> 議論の組み立てには，信頼できる情報が必要である．現在では，情報が見つからないということは少なく，むしろWebや書籍など，さまざまなところに情報が存在している．この章では数多く存在する情報源の中から，学術的な議論に耐えうる確かな情報源の探し方を学ぶ．また，情報源を見つけたら，議論に相応しい情報を選択しなければならない．入手した情報から持論をどのようにサポートするのか，その方法についても見ていこう．

In Part I of this book you learned that your academic community challenges you to pose and consider serious, relevant, and significant questions. Ideally, these questions should inspire you to construct, develop, and support an argument that evolves from a research question. To construct that argument, you need to synthesize pieces of academic evidence from *credible* sources; that is, trustworthy and believable sources of information. The first step, obviously, is to find good sources of information. Once you have a credible source, you need to select the information that is most useful for supporting your argument. After that, you must put the information into your paper. In addition, you have to make sure that you have credible support for each of the major points of your argument. This chapter is designed to help you with these aspects of researching an academic paper.

1. Finding sources

1.1 Sources of information

We live in the age of the ubiquitous Internet, and today many people immediately begin searching for information by using a computer and a Web search engine such as Yahoo! or Google.

Learning Task 1

Web sites are one source of information, what are some others? Make a list below.

```
            SOURCES OF INFORMATION

    • Internet Web sites
    •
    •
    •
    •
    •
```

1.2 Using keywords to find information

The keywords that you use for your search are very important. A good keyword can help you find many sources of potentially useful information. A poor keyword can frustrate you by delivering very little information. Consider your keywords carefully and do not give up too quickly. Research takes time.

Learning Task 2

With your own research question in mind, find credible information sources by using three search methods: an online library catalog search, a general Internet search, and an academic Internet search. If you do not yet have your own research question, or you would just like to practice finding information, use this research question: *What are some possible effects of the lay judge system in Japan?*

1.3 Online library catalog search

Learning Task 3

Go to your library's Internet homepage. Find the online library catalog and enter the English keywords of your research question.

Search number	English Keywords (vary keywords each time)	Number of Sources Generated (list the sources that seem best)	Search Quality
1.			__ good __ average __ poor
2.			__ good __ average __ poor
3.			__ good __ average __ poor

Learning Task 4

Search again, but this time, translate the search terms to Japanese. If you are not satisfied with the amount or quality of your information, search again with slightly different keywords.

Search number	Japanese Keywords (vary keywords each time)	Number of Sources Generated (list the sources that seem best)	Search Quality
1.			__ good __ average __ poor
2.			__ good __ average __ poor
3.			__ good __ average __ poor

1.4 General internet search

Learning Task 5

Do an Internet search with a search engine such as Yahoo! or Google with the same English keywords that you used above in your online library catalog search.

Search number	Keywords	Number of Sources Generated (list the sources that seem best)	Search Quality
1.			__ good __ average __ poor

Learning Task 6

Check the language preference setting on your search engine. Are you searching Japanese Web pages or English Web pages? Search again, but this time, change the language preferences to either Japanese or English (whichever one is different from your original search).

Search number	Keywords (Japanese ⇄ English)	Number of Sources Generated (list the sources that seem best)	Search Quality
2.			__ good __ average __ poor

Learning Task 7

Are the search results the same for both language preferences? If not, how are they different? What type of sources appeared in the search results in English compared to the search results in Japanese?

1.5 Google scholar search

Google Scholar is a Web search engine for academic literature, especially academic journal articles.

Learning Task 8

Go to Google Scholar (http://scholar.google.com/) and search for information with the same keywords you used for your searches above.

Search number	Keywords	Number of Sources Generated (list the sources that seem best)	Search Quality
1.			__ good __ average __ poor

Learning Task 9

Search again, but this time, change the language preferences to either Japanese or English (whichever one is different from your original search).

Search number	Keywords (Japanese ⇄ English)	Number of Sources Generated (list the sources that seem best)	Search Quality
2.			__ good __ average __ poor

Learning Task 10

Are the search results the same for both language preferences? If not, how are they different? Which search do you think provided the best quality information?

2. Primary and secondary sources

Sources can be categorized into two general categories: *secondary sources* and *primary sources*. The type of sources that are likely more familiar to you such as books, encyclopedias, newspapers, and magazines are called secondary sources because they usually rely on another type of source of information; namely, primary sources of information (e.g., research papers).

Primary sources of information such as research papers usually involve a *peer review* process; that is, before a paper is published, other knowledgeable scholars read the work and provide criticisms and comments. Through the process of peer review, a manuscript submitted to be published in the primary literature is improved through a discussion between the writer, reviewer, and the editor of the academic journal. Indeed, it may be comforting for you to know that academic writing is a difficult and time-consuming process even for your professors. Every scholar sometimes receives harsh criticisms of their work and must re-write papers several times before they can be published in professional journals.

3. Evaluating the credibility of sources

How and where will you find credible sources for your paper? What is an appropriate way to use freely accessible and editable online encyclopedias such as the Wikipedia? This section addresses questions such as these.

Regardless of the type of sources of information you decide to use for your academic paper, it is important to carefully evaluate the credibility of your sources. To do this, you may begin by asking and answering questions such as those in Table 7.1.

3.1 Evaluating general Internet search results

In Figure 7.1 are search results generated on the Internet for the research question, *What will be the effects of the lay judge system in Japan?* Included are the top results of a general Internet search using Google in English with the following keywords: *lay, judge,* and *Japan.*

Table 7.1 Questions to Evaluate the Credibility of a Source of Information

Who?	Who is/are the author(s)?
	Where does the author work?
	What is the author's reputation?
Where?	Where is the information published? (e.g., blog, book, newspaper)
	Who is the publisher?
	Are there any biases inherent in the source?
When?	When was the information published?
	Is it a recent, outdated or classic source?
	In what sort of historical, social, and cultural context was the information written?
What?	What do you think was the motivation of the author(s) for writing this material?
	What is the importance of this material?

Google   lay judge japan   Search   Advanced Search

Web   ⊞Show options...   Results

Juries in **Japan** - Wikipedia, the free encyclopedia
Newly instituted **Japanese** system is unique in that the panel of six **lay judges**, chosen randomly from the public, together with three professional **judges**, ...
New law - First jury trial under new law - References - External links
en.wikipedia.org/wiki/Juries_in_Japan - Cached - Similar -

Lay judge law to start May 21 next year | The **Japan** Times Online
9 Apr 2008 ... The law establishing the **lay judge** system, in which citizens will serve as de facto jurors in trials involving serious crimes, ...
search.**japan**times.co.jp/cgi-bin/nn20080409a2.html - Similar -

Lay judges? No thanks! | 世論 What **Japan** Thinks
22 Jan 2006 ... Last August, Central Research Services, Inc performed a survey regarding the introduction of **lay judges** to the **Japanese** judicial system by ...
what**japan**thinks.com/2006/01/22/**lay-judges**-no-thanks/ - Cached - Similar -

Figure 7.1 General Google Search Top Results

Learning Task 11

Use the table below to identify each of the three sources in Figure 7.1.

Source 1 Title:	Type of source: (e.g., journal, blog)	__ credible __ not credible reason:
Source 2 Title:	Type of source:	__ credible __ not credible reason:
Source 3 Title:	Type of source:	__ credible __ not credible reason:

Learning Task 12

Do this search yourself using the same keywords. Find these Web pages, and evaluate the credibility of the sources by answering the questions in Table 7.1 above.

4. Making use of Wikipedia[1] in academic papers

Are you familiar with the source of information for the first result listed in Figure 7.1? Of course, it is the Wikipedia, an online encyclopedia that is free to access and also free to edit by anyone in the world. Please remember that information written in the Wikipedia should **not** be used as a source of information for your academic papers. This is because the authors of Wikipedia articles are almost impossible to identify so no one can be held accountable for the information; in other words, the Wikipedia *lacks credibility*. Despite this, however, the Wikipedia can be a useful source of ideas. How can you use a Wikipedia article for your academic research paper? One way is to use the Wikipedia as a place to find secondary or even primary sources of information on a certain topic.

Learning Task 13

Look at the Wikipedia article, "Juries in Japan" (http://en.wikipedia.org/wiki/Juries_in_Japan; accessed on 4 October 2009): At the end of most Wikipedia articles is a section called *References*. Look at Figure 7.2 to see the reference list for the article, "Juries in Japan."

References   [edit]

1. ^ Ingram Weber, The New Japanese Jury System: Empowering the Public, Preserving Continental Justice, 4 East Asia Law Review 125 (2009)
2. ^ [a] [b] Tabuchi, Hiroko; McDonald, Mark (August 6, 2009), "In First Return to Japan Court, Jurors Convict and Sentence", *New York Times*, retrieved 2009-08-06
3. ^ "Japan's landmark jury trial ends", *BBC News*, August 6, 2009, retrieved 2009-08-06
4. ^ Wallacy, Mark (August 6, 2009), "Japan revives jury trials", *ABC News*, retrieved 2009-08-06
5. ^ [McCurry, Justin] (August 3, 2009), "Trial by jury returns to Japan Thousands queue to witness historic change to country's criminal justice syste", *Guardian.co.uk*, retrieved 2009-08-06
6. ^ Onishi, Norimitsu (2007-07-16). "Japan Learns Dreaded Task of Jury Duty". *New York Times*. Retrieved 2007-07-16.

Figure 7.2 Reference List for a Wikipedia Article

Learning Task 14

Identify the secondary and primary sources in this reference list. Choose one secondary source and one primary source and try to locate them using the online library catalog, a general Internet search, or a Google Scholar search. Evaluate the credibility of these sources by answering the questions in Table 7.1. Discuss your evaluation of the two sources with classmates.

Primary sources:	Secondary sources:
One Primary Source:	Evaluation: __ credible __ not credible – reason:
One Secondary Source:	Evaluation: __ credible __ not credible – reason:

4.1 Example of a Google Scholar search

Learning Task 15

Figure 7.3 shows the top results of a Google Scholar search using the same keywords as the general Internet (Google) search. What are the similarities and differences of the search results? Discuss them with a classmate.

```
Google scholar  [lay judge japan]  (Search)   Advanced Scholar Search
                                              Scholar Preferences

Scholar  All articles  Recent articles

[CITATION] Top Court Notifying Lay Judge Candidates
S Kamiya - Japan Times, November, 2008
Cited by 3

[PDF] ▶ Testing Japan's Convictions: The Lay Judge System and the Rights of Criminal Defendants
AF Soldwedel - Vanderbilt Journal of Transnational Law - law.vanderbilt.edu
... Ct. of Japan, SAIBANIN SENIN TETSUZUKI NO GAIYO [Outline of Lay Judge Selection
Process], available at http://www.saibanin.courts.go.jp/shiryo/pdf/09.pdf). 46. ...
Cited by 3 - View as HTML

[CITATION] Face of the Lay Judge System (Editorial)
J Times - Japan Times, February, 2007
Cited by 1

[PDF] ▶ Judicial Precedents Processing Project for Supporting Japanese Lay Judge System
R Rzepka, H Shibuki, Y Kimura, K Takamaru, ... - Workshop Programme - lrec-conf.org
... paper we introduced our idea of a supporting tool for law amateurs who will be selected
randomly in Japan from May 2009 to become a" lay judge", a specific ...
Cited by 1 - Related articles - View as HTML

[CITATION] Politicians Worried by Lay Judge System form Nonpartisan Group to Delay it
S Kamiya - Japan Times, April, 20
Cited by 1

[PDF] ▶ ... participation in the lay judge system (Saiban'in seido) of Japan?: an interaction effect ...
E Yamamura - 2009 - mpra.ub.uni-muenchen.de
... II. OVERVIEW OF THE LAY JUDGE SYSTEM IN JAPAN A. The lay judge system ... (JSRC 2001,
Chapter I Part1). Contrary to the premise, the lay judge system in Japan ...
View as HTML
```

Figure 7.3 Google Scholar Search Results

5. Selecting information

Once you have a book, article or chapter that you think will be a useful source for your research, you must choose the information most relevant for your academic paper topic. You do not have enough time normally to read several books and articles from beginning to end. This section will give you some advice about how to save time finding the information you need in sources.

5.1 Books

Part I of this book contains information on how to read a text for details that apply to a specific topic. How can you find the information you need without reading all of Part I?

- Check the Table of Contents
- Check the Index

Learning Task 16

What information do you see in the Table of Contents of this book? The chapter titles should give you some idea about where you might begin. Which chapter(s) would you look at first? Why? What are the important keywords?

Chapter(s):	Keywords:

If the Table of Contents does not help you and the book has an index, check the index. An index is a list of keywords arranged in alphabetical order. Which keyword(s) would you search for in the index? If there is no index, or you cannot find your keywords listed in the index, what will you do? Here is some advice:

- Check the chapter headings

Do not read the entire chapter from beginning to end. Instead you should scan the chapter headings for your keywords. The title of Chapter 5 has two important keywords for this search: *reading* and *application*. Our topic relates to academic reading, but a theoretical approach is not the specific concern. This topic is specifically about how to apply theory in practice. The keywords listed after the abstract are helpful too. Heading 1 does not help us much. Heading 2 is promising. If you scan to Heading 3, you should immediately see that this section is about the four techniques used in reading academic texts.

> **Learning Task 17**
>
> Write definitions for the following terms. Use your own words and give examples, if possible.
>
> *Scanning:*
>
> *Skimming:*
>
> *Skipping:*
>
> *Diving:*

5.2 Academic journals

Academic journals have a list of contents, but most do not have indexes, although some journals publish keyword indexes at the end of each volume year. This means that you must carefully consider the title, keyword list (if there is one), abstract, headings, tables and figures to find the specific information related to your topic. How do you do this? You locate text that is useful for your particular purpose through: scanning, skimming, skipping and diving. See Chapter 5 for a detailed discussion of these important academic reading techniques.

5.2.1 Taking notes and listing sources

You must keep a record of every information source that you use to write your paper for two reasons. First, when you do research you often look at many sources. This makes it very easy to forget where the information is from. Second, it is easy to mix up sources when working on larger writing projects so good record keeping can save you a lot of time. In short, try to be organized and systematic when you do academic research.

Learning Task 18

What advice does Chapter 5 of this book offer on this point? Find the specific section of Chapter 5, review it and then discuss the points with classmates. Which of these points do you do now when studying?

6. Assessing information

Learning Task 19

Now that you have gathered and read some information for your academic paper, it is time to see how well your information supports the main points of your argument. Use the table below to help you assess if you have the appropriate information for your paper.

Thesis statement:		
Main Point:	Sources of support:	Page numbers/sections:
Main Point:	Sources of support:	Page numbers/sections:
Main Point:	Sources of support:	Page numbers/sections:
Main Point:	Sources of support:	Page numbers/sections:

Your main points might change as you read more about the topic of your research. If you do not have adequate support for a main point, you need to try to find additional sources. Again, it is essential for you to keep records of the sources that you use in your academic papers.

7. Using sources

Now that you have found credible information for your academic paper, what should you do with it? As discussed in the opening section of this book, the university is a part of an academic culture in which people share core values and beliefs. The way in which people communicate through writing at the university is also based on these values and beliefs. Though it is certainly true that professors in the sciences, for example, communicate research findings through writing in ways that are different from how professors in the arts do, all academics, regardless of their discipline, place a high value on theory, logic, and evidence-based arguments. In addition, they believe that it is important to build on previous academic work. Therefore, depending on the writing assignment, professors often expect their students to acknowledge the work of scholars in their writing.

The following three skills are related to acknowledging and building on the previous work of others: *summarizing, paraphrasing,* and *quoting.* Using these academic writing skills, you can identify and give credit to sources of information. This process is called *citation;* to cite is the act of identifying specific sources of information that are used in an academic paper. Let us now consider quoting, paraphrasing, and summarizing in detail.

7.1 Quoting

Why use quotations? When you read a source and find important words and passages central to your argument that are written by an acknowledged expert, it is sometimes best not to change these words. If you copy text directly from a source this is called a quotation. There are two basic types of quotations, short and long.

7.1.1 Short quotations
Short quotations are incorporated into the body of a paragraph. If the section of text you select to quote is 25 words or less, you can write a short quotation inside quotation marks. Here is an example of a short quotation.

> Stewart (2009) claims, "It is essential that language policy goals are realistic, consistent and accurately reflect student needs and teacher capabilities" (p. 11). But what does he mean by "realistic"? A realistic language policy goal is very difficult to define. In the next section of this paper, I will attempt to formulate such a definition for the context of Japanese junior and senior high schools.

What are the parts of this short quotation?

- First, the author and source are cited (Stewart, 2009). This information could come at the end of a quotation. Why is the author's name not inside the brackets?
- Second, the quote is introduced with a reporting verb (claims). Note that the reporting verb is followed by a comma. Some other common reporting verbs are: *report, state, say, declare,* and *explain*.
- Third, the quotation is written. Following the comma are quotation marks that show where the quotation begins. At the end of the quotation there are marks that show where it ends. They are followed by a space, the page number in the source text (p. 11) and a period. Make sure that you copy the exact words when you use quotations.
- Fourth, the content of the quotation is commented on. Do not simply string a line of important sounding quotes together in your paper. Each quotation needs to have a significant meaning for your topic. That means you have to comment on the significance of each of your quotes. If you do not feel the need to comment on a quotation, then you should not include it in your academic paper.

Here is another example of a short quote, taken from Chapter 1 of this book:

> Academic writing addresses "general" (interdisciplinary) as well as "specific" (within a discipline) audiences. There are also various genres of academic writing; e.g., essays, course term reports, examination answers, book reviews, research papers, and graduate school dissertations. Swales (1990, p. 58) provides a clear definition of genre by stating, "A genre comprises a class of communicative events, the members of which share some set [sic–*some set* means *a set*] of communicative purposes". In this book, our genre (i.e., the class of communicative events) of interest is the research paper; the shared public purpose is to present a written report of new research; and the participants are members of the academic community of all people interested in the findings of that particular research.

In the example above, you can see how the author used words directly from a leading theorist in applied linguistics in order to provide the reader with an authoritative definition of *genre*. Here you should notice three things: 1) the use of quotations marks before the definition and after the definition, 2) the reporting of the author's name, date of the source of the material, and the page number of the source of the material, and 3) the quotation is inside the paragraph. All of these elements are necessary when you write a short quotation.

Learning Task 20

What page is the above passage on? Challenge a classmate to scan for it and see who can find it first.

7.1.2 Long quotations

Long quotations are separated from paragraphs. Quotation marks are not used for long quotations.

Here is an example:

> With a deep sense of pessimism, *The Japan Times* labeled the new curriculum for 2013 to be "too little too late":
>
> > This conversion from traditional methods to a more active and communicative approach is decades behind the rest of the world. As China, Vietnam and South Korea have moved ahead, Japan's English education policies have languished. It may be a case of too little too late. Japan's position in the future internationalized world will be determined by the nation's English ability. ("English taught in English," 2009)

What are the parts of this long quotation?

- First, the quotation is introduced and starts after the colon (:).
- Second, the long quotation is separated from the paragraph. The left margin is adjusted inward for the entire quotation.
- Third, quotation marks are not used.
- Fourth, the period comes before the citation. This source is a newspaper article for which the author is not indicated. Therefore, the article title is in quotation marks.

Learning Task 21

Skim Part I of this book for three minutes. How many long quotations can you find?

7.2 Paraphrasing

In an academic paper, you cannot quote everything that you read. If your paper contains a lot of long quotations, it likely means that you are simply copying material. Copying does not involve a lot of thinking. In Chapter 4, you learned about critical thinking and critical reading. You can practice them through selective quotation, paraphrasing, and summarizing.

Paraphrasing involves putting the essential part of some piece of information into your own words. When you paraphrase, you rephrase or rewrite information that was previously published. You normally paraphrase one or two sentences, or perhaps a paragraph.

Important points about paraphrasing:

- Select short sections to paraphrase.
- State the ideas from the original text in your own words.
- Include all of the information from the original text in your paraphrase.
- Do not change the meaning of the original text.

Learning Task 22

Consider the difference between the original source material and paraphrased version of the source material in Example 1 and write the changes in the table below.

Example 1

Original
The higher education system of the United States is widely admired even though approximately half of the undergraduate students who enroll in American universities actually get a bachelor's degree. The only other Organisation for Economic Co-operation and Development country with a poorer record is Italy.

Paraphrase sample
Even though people around the world admire American universities, only half of the teenagers enrolled in university in the United States graduate. Italy is the only other OECD country with a worse record.

Write the changes to the original text in the center column.

Original text	Paraphrased text	Type of change
even though	Even though	sentence position
is widely admired		passive form to active form
The higher education system of the United States		synonym
approximately		synonym
undergraduate students		synonym
enroll		word form
American		word form
get a bachelor's degree		synonym
is Italy		sentence position
Organisation for Economic Co-operation and Development		(word) form
poorer		synonym

For these two short sentences eleven changes were made. You do not necessarily need to make so many changes, but carefully consider the changes that you do make. For example, consider the change from *approximately* to *only*. Is this an accurate change?

Choosing synonyms can sometimes be difficult. *Only* means "at most, barely, just," whereas *approximately* is defined as "nearly, about, around or roughly." These two words are not synonyms. The adverb *approximately* is an amount within a limited range of possibility, but *only* is an adverb signifying a definite amount.

Learning Task 23

Take a look at the change from *undergraduates* to *teenagers* and consider how accurate it is. Discuss this point with classmates.

Example 2

> *Paraphrased Text in Chapter 3*
> Receptive vocabulary knowledge is related to comprehending meaning from a particular word form in reading and listening, while productive vocabulary knowledge is related to conveying meaning by using an appropriate word form in writing and speaking (Nation, 2001).

The author of Chapter 3 consulted a lot of sources, including Paul Nation's 2001 publication. In this paraphrase of Nation (2001) note again, how the original source material is given credit like this: (Family name, year). This information allows the reader to identify the source.

Learning Task 24

What type of publication is Nation 2001 (e.g., academic journal article, book, book chapter, Web site, newspaper article)? Please locate this reference in Chapter 3.

Learning Task 25

Paraphrase Practice

Directions
- Read the original text more than once and make sure that you understand it.
- Look for synonyms for the words you think are important.
- Write the sentences again: simplify the structure and use synonyms.
- Read your paraphrase and be sure that it contains all of the information contained in the original text. Do not change the meaning of the original passage.
- Ask a classmate to check your work and compare ideas.

> *Original*
> In academia, plagiarism by students, researchers or professors is considered academic dishonesty or academic fraud and offenders are subject to censure, up to and including expulsion. Since plagiarism is the reproduction of ideas, words or statements of someone else without due acknowledgement, students should be sure to cite all important ideas and words taken from sources.

Follow the directions above and write your paraphrase.

7.3 Summarizing

Summarizing is similar to paraphrasing, but you summarize longer pieces of text, even entire articles. Of course, you must also paraphrase (i.e., use your own words) whenever you write a summary. Unlike paraphrases, summaries do not include all of the information in the original text. When you prepare a summary of source material, you must first decide what the main points are. Summaries are much shorter than the original text.

Consider the following excerpt from Chapter 2 of this book as an example of how to use a summary in a research paper.

> The notions of "move" and "step" (Swales, 1990) will be particularly useful in helping you learn about the structure of research articles. The term "move" refers to a component of a paper that serves a particular communicative function and purpose. For example, if part of the text in an *Introduction* section of a paper is a single unit because it describes the work in the paper, it would be identified as a "move." One "move" may consist of smaller units called "steps." If part of the "move" that describes the work in the paper states an outcome of the research, that part is referred to as one "step" of the "move."

The author of the original source, Swales, has written a great deal about what he calls "move analysis." This short section of text from Chapter 2 is a summary of the main points of Swales' ideas that are useful to the argument put forward in Chapter 2 of this book. The author likely read Swales' publications and thought about these ideas for some time before writing this summary.

Notice how credit is given to the author who wrote the original material (i.e., Swales) and the year in which the material was published (i.e., 1990). This is called an *in-text citation*. With this information, it is possible for the reader to identify the source of the information by referring to the references section at the end of the paper, which contains *reference citations* corresponding to the in-text citations.

Write out the full reference citation for this publication here:

Please see Chapter 12 for more details about citation using the American Psychological Association (APA) style guide.

7.3.1 Guidelines for summarizing

Step 1: Read the original text until you understand it.
Step 2: Underline main ideas and the important details.
Step 3: Begin your rough notes by rewriting (paraphrase) what you underlined.
Step 4: Paraphrase the text further and put it into your own words. Here is a review of the four most common paraphrasing techniques:
  a. Insert synonyms
     Original: The human brain is complex.
     Paraphrase: The human brain has many intricate details.
  b. Use different word forms
     Original: Experience is our teacher.
     Paraphrase: Experience teaches us.

c. Change active to passive, or vice versa
   Original: Culture is learned.
   Paraphrase: People learn about their culture.
d. Change negative to affirmative, or vice versa
   Original: No person is unaffected by culture.
   Paraphrase: Everyone is affected by culture.

Step 5: Write from your handwritten notes.

Learning Task 26

Read the short passage below and correct the errors. There are at least eight. After that, follow the guidelines above and write a summary of the passage.

> …The key to writing something that has of reasonable quality is to start writing. Off course, research, background reading and planning are all important aspect of the academic writing process, but you cannot stop there. Many people have difficulty getting started in projects. It appears to be very easy, and more fun, to avoid assignments. In English, we can call this behaving procrastination. The verb procrastinate breaks down neatly onto two main parts. The root "cras" means tomorrow and the prefix "pro" means to favour. This combination gives us a word with a meaning that is the antithesis of an English proverb, Don't *put off to tomorrow what you can do today.* This sounds rather austere in its efficiency and no doubt has been told by many teachers and parents to their "lazy" children over the years. One of the most famous procrastinators in history is said to have been the great Leonardo da Vinci. Apparently, he needs strict deadlines to inspire him to finish his many projects, including threats to have his hands chopped off. Thus, one way to avoid procrastination is to set your own realistic deadlines for writing assignments and, most importantly, meat them. If you don't you might receive a poor grade, but your hands should remain attached to your arms.

Learning Task 27

Choose a section of a chapter in Part I of this book that interests you and write a summary of it.

Note

1 A couple of alternatives to the Wikipedia that are freely accessible, peer-reviewed, and credible online encyclopedias are Scholarpedia (http://www.scholarpedia.org/) and the Stanford Encyclopedia of Philosophy (http://plato.stanford.edu/). Also see Chapter 15 for additional information sources.

───── この章のまとめ

信頼できる情報源を見つけることはできただろうか．また，現在では，情報を見つけることよりも，より確かな情報を見極める方が重要である．情報の使い方として，引用や要約についても学習した．情報を上手に使いこなすことは，学術的議論に限らず重要なので，しっかりと身につけておきたい．

Chapter 8　Writing the Abstract

> **この章のねらい**
> この章では，abstract（抄録）の作成方法を学ぶ．abstract は，学術論文においてタイトルの次に読まれる箇所である．現在，さまざまな学術論文誌が刊行されているが，すべての論文が等しく読まれるわけではない．読者の興味を集めるためには，論文の内容が過不足なく伝わる abstract を準備する必要がある．ここでは，実際の文章を元にして，どのように abstract を作り上げていくかを見ていこう．

An abstract provides readers with the purpose of the study, the method, and the main results. To be more precise, an abstract is defined as follows: "They [research article abstracts] function as stand-alone mini-texts, giving readers a short summary of a study's topic, methodology, and main findings" (Huckin, 2001, as cited in Swales & Feak, 2009, p. 2).

In addition to an abstract for a research article, there are also abstracts for master's theses and doctoral dissertations. Besides these, there is also an abstract for a conference proposal. If you want to present your study at a conference, you need to write an abstract (also called a *conference proposal*) and send it to the conference organizing committee for approval.

1. Background

1.1 When do you write an abstract?

In the case of writing abstracts for research articles, master's theses and doctoral dissertations, you write an abstract when you finish your study or at the point when you know the main results of the study. In the case of an abstract for a conference presentation, however, you can write it even before you finish your study. In that case, you still need to include the information about the main results you will expect from the study.

1.2 Why is an abstract important?

From the definition of an abstract provided above, you understand that by reading an abstract you can get an overall idea about what the study is about. Moreover, an abstract gives you an idea about whether you want to read the entire article, thesis or dissertation. When you do your own study, you need to search for information relevant to your topic. This process is called a *literature review*. When you do a literature review, in many cases, you have limited time, and thus, by reading abstracts you can determine whether the paper is relevant to your study and worth reading. In fact, these functions of abstracts, those of research articles in particular, are defined as "*screening devices,* helping readers decide whether they wish to read the whole article or not" and "*previews* for readers intending to read the whole article, giving them a road-map for their reading" (Huckin, 2001, as cited in Swales & Feak, 2009, p. 2).

1.3 Why can writing a good abstract be difficult?

Now you understand why an abstract is important, but it is not easy to write. The most difficult part in writing an abstract is that you have to stay within a word limit. Usually, journals set a word limit for an abstract, such as 150 words or 200 words. Based on the data from Orasan (2001, as cited in Swales & Feak, 2009), the overall average number of words for research article abstracts from various fields is 175. To give you an idea about word count, the abstract in Chapter 2 of this book has 163 words. In writing an abstract, you will encounter a difficult task of putting the necessary information in a limited amount of words and at the same time draw readers' attention. Many researchers find it difficult to write a good abstract. Being able to write a clear abstract takes practice.

Learning Task 1

Look back at the chapters in Part I of this book. Just after the title, you will see a short paragraph that comes before the main text. This is called an *abstract*. Read one of the chapter abstracts in Part I again. What kind of information does it contain? Discuss this with a classmate.

2. Practice writing an abstract

In order to write an abstract, you have to have a complete paper. An abstract is usually written to outline a study of the research you conduct. To begin here, you will first practice with an easier piece of writing, instead of a research article. Read the sample academic paper below written by a Japanese undergraduate and then go through the steps to write an abstract for this paper.

2.1 Sample student paper

The following sample uses a cause and effect organization. Cause and effect is one of the rhetorical modes (see Chapter 10) used in English for General Academic Purposes (EGAP) papers. A cause and effect paper deals with results or phenomena and the analyses of their possible causes. The research question is likely to be something like, *Why did X occur?* For more on the cause and effect pattern, see Chapter 10.

The following essay was written by a Japanese first-year student of Kyoto University. The student, who was interested in Japanese animation, chose to investigate the reasons behind the popularity of a song from a Japanese TV animation program. Although she did research on her topic, references are not included because at this stage in the class students had not yet learned how to cite sources in academic papers.

"Happy Material"

"Happy Material" is a song, which was used as an opening song for a TV animation "Magical Teacher Negima." This animation was telecasted in Japan from January 6, 2005 to June 29, 2005. This animation describes a 10-year-old boy who becomes an English teacher at a girls' school. He takes charge of 3–A. This class has 31 students. "Happy Material" was sung by the students of this class. Although the actual singers were radio actresses, this song was sold in the name of the characters. This song had seven versions. Version 4 ranked third in Oricon hit chart and ranked twentieth in World Single Chart. There are four reasons why "Happy Material" sold well.

The first reason was that the price of this CD was very cheap. This CD sold for 735 yen each. In addition, despite its low price, one character card was attached to the first limited edition of this CD. Therefore, not only grown-ups who had earnings but also children who only had pocket money were able to buy this CD.

The second reason was that the radio actresses of all characters of this animation were decided by the audition. For example, radio actresses were required to read four dialogues aloud in the audition. Many popular radio actresses such as Masumi Asano failed in this audition. On the other hand, 10 out of 31 radio actresses were new figures. It was an unprecedented action that 31 radio actresses were determined by the audition. When characters of one animation are too many, one radio actress usually takes charge of two or three characters' voices. That's because the budget is limited and some characters have few dialogues. However, this animation decided 31 radio actresses who voiced each character. As a result of this audition, the voices of the radio actresses fit very well with the characters' images, so many consumers bought this CD.

The third reason was that this CD had seven versions. It was exceptional that seven kinds of CDs based on the same melody were released. These seven kinds of CDs were released consecutively for seven months. This song was sung by six groups which were made by the division of 3–A. For example, version 1 of this CD was sung by six students whose attendance numbers were from 1 to 6 and was used as an opening song of this animation in January, 2005. In the same way, version 2 was sung by five students whose attendance numbers were from 7 to 11 and was used as an opening song of this animation in February, 2005. Similarly, versions 3, 4, 5, 6 were released. Version 7 was released after the end of this animation. This was sung by all students of 3-A. This version was used as an opening song of the last story. The TV viewers of this animation were interested in this song because of its diversity. However, if a difference of these seven kinds of CDs was only the members who sang the song, this song didn't become a hit song. Sumiko Shindo who took charge of this animation's music thought that a minor change of each CD wouldn't attract attention from the public, so she aimed at large changes of these CDs. That is why she changed arrangement and the lyrics of this song. These devices led to the induction of customers' interest.

However, the most important reason for the strong sales of "Happy Material" was purchase activity of the fans. For example, when version 4 of this song ranked third in Oricon hit chart, some enthusiastic fans of this animation made thread which supported "Happy Material" as an Internet forum. This thread's name was "Super-fast VIPPER thread." That's why the users of this thread were called VIPPER. They wanted "Happy Material" to rank first. Even though character songs have a good sale, they are not picked up much on TV and in the newspaper. When worst comes to worst, their existence is ignored in Japanese music industry. VIPPER thought that if "Happy Material" ranked first, the news media couldn't avoid picking up this song. They tried to start a revolution against the ruined Japanese music industry. They organized a band to spread "Happy Material" and threw many concerts in various areas. Their home page recommended many fans to buy this CD at the specialty stores of Oricon hit chart. This purchase activity resulted from dissatisfaction with Japanese music industry. Many people who saw their activity began to cooperate with VIPPER by purchasing this CD. Their activity was reported on TV and in the newspaper. Their enthusiastic purchase activity contributed to the hit of this song.

For these reasons, many people bought this CD and "Happy Material" had good sales.

Note: Minor changes were made to the student's paper for this chapter.

2.2 Guidelines for writing an abstract

Write an abstract for the cause and effect paper "Happy Material" using the six steps.

Step 1: Identifying the main ideas
Think of an abstract as being similar to a summary. Keeping this in mind, you need to select the main points of the paper. Use the questions below to help you.

   a. What is this paper about?
   b. What does the author try to do in this paper?
   c. What are the main results?

The answer to the first question is, of course, "Happy Material." The answer to the second question is that the author tries to analyze the reasons for the good sales of "Happy Material." Finally, the author found four reasons for the good sales, which are the main results.

Step 2: Highlighting significant background information
After identifying the main points, you have to think about the audience reading this paper. Since you have read the entire paper, you know what "Happy Material" is. However, you have to assume that readers do not know anything about this topic. Thus, in the beginning, you should outline necessary background information about the topic. Use the questions below to help you.

   a. What is "Happy Material"?
   b. Why is "Happy Material" worth investigating?

The answer to the first question is in the first sentence of the essay: *"Happy Material" is a song, which was used as an opening song for a TV animation "Magical Teacher Negima".* This animation was telecasted in Japan from January 6, 2005 to June 29, 2005. The answer to the second question as to why it is worth writing about is that this song sold well; among the seven versions of this song, Version 4 ranked third on the Oricon Hit Chart and ranked twentieth in the World Single Chart.

Step 3: Summarizing the main results
The main results are easy to find because the author makes a clear thesis statement: *There are four reasons why "Happy Material" sold well.* In addition, the author guides readers to the four reasons by using such phrases as "The first reason was …" "The second reason was …" and so forth. Look at the paper again and

write the four reasons below.

> Reason 1:
>
> Reason 2:
>
> Reason 3:
>
> Reason 4:

Step 4: Writing a good concluding sentence

After summarizing the main results, you need a concluding sentence to end the abstract. Usually a concluding sentence begins with such phrases as "in conclusion," "in short," or "in summary." In addition, you need to restate the main results in a concise way.

Step 5: Staying within the word limit

Now that you understand what information should be included in the abstract, you need to think more specifically about how you write the abstract. As mentioned earlier, an abstract usually has a word limit, such as 150 words or 200 words. Thus, you have to use words precisely. Moreover, you may need to think about eliminating some information, although you first considered it necessary.

It will also be necessary to condense information in order to use fewer words. For example, earlier we answered the questions, *What is "Happy Material?"* and *Why is it worth discussing in this essay?* in the following way:

> "Happy Material" is a song, which was used as an opening song for a TV animation "Magical Teacher Negima." This animation was telecasted in Japan from January 6, 2005 to June 29, 2005. Among the seven versions of this song, Version 4 ranked third in Oricon hit chart and ranked twentieth in the World Single Chart.

If you write the above passage in your abstract, your abstract will probably be too long. Besides, you may not need all the detailed information in the abstract. For example, the song ranking third in the Oricon Hit Chart and ranking twentieth in the World Single Chart can be simply described as "an unusual success." Thus, the passage above can be shortened in the following way:

> "Happy Material," an opening song for a TV animation "Magical Teacher Negima," broadcast in 2005, made unusual success in CD sales as an animation song.

Step 6: Paraphrase and write the abstract in your own words

Learning Task 2

Review Steps 1–5 and then read the paper "Happy Material" again. Write an abstract for this paper in your own words. Try to aim for a word limit of 150 words.

2.3 Proofreading your abstract

How clear was your abstract? Answer the following questions:

a. Did you find writing the abstract easy or difficult? If difficult, what was the most difficult part?
b. How many words did you write? Were you able to stay within the 150-word limit? If not, which part of your abstract do you think you could have shortened?

In order to give you an idea about where you could have improved in your abstract, here is one model that you could follow:

Model abstract

> "Happy Material"
>
> "Happy Material," an opening song for a TV animation "Magical Teacher Negima," broadcast in 2005, made unusual success in CD sales as an animation song. The following four reasons contributed to its success. First, the CD was inexpensive. Second, 31 voice actresses who played the voices of the 31 female characters in the story, sang the song. Third, seven different versions of this song, sung by different groups of the 31 voice actresses, were released consecutively. Finally, the most important reason was various activities by enthusiastic fans of this song. In order to increase the sales of this CD and draw the media's attention, the fans opened a website and formed a band to advertize this song through the Internet and concerts. In conclusion, a combination of various factors brought great success to the song "Happy Material." (138 words)

Learning Task 3

Review this chapter and write an abstract for your paper. Ask a classmate to read it and give you comments.

References

Swales, J. M., & Feak, C. B. (2009). *Abstracts and the writing of abstracts.* Ann Arbor: The University of Michigan Press.

───── この章のまとめ

abstract の重要性は理解できただろうか．どんなによい内容の研究を行ったり，学術論文を書き上げたりしても，読者に読んでもらえなければ意味がない．abstract は論文の一部であるとともに，論文を代表する顔でもある．要点の絞り込み方や，過不足のない abstract の条件は理解できただろうか．

Chapter 9 Writing the Introduction

> **この章のねらい**
> この章では，introduction（導入部）の作成方法を学ぶ．introduction は，多くの分野の学術論文において共通の役割を担っている．introduction の役割は，読者に論文の見取り図を提供することである．また，同時に論文の位置づけを示すものでもある．研究や論文の背景を読者に伝え，論文の重要性を理解してもらわなくてはならない．したがって，導入の方法も一般的なことから始まって，より具体的な問題の説明へ展開する形をとる．ここでは，前章の題材や新聞記事を元に，introduction の作成方法と形式について見ていこう．

In this chapter, you will learn how to write the first section of an academic paper, the introduction. First, you need to understand what role the introduction plays in an academic paper.

In the previous chapter, you learned how to write an abstract. An abstract provides readers with a quick overview of a study. However, an abstract is a separate text from the main text. The introduction introduces your topic, gives readers an idea about the organization of the paper, and outlines the main points of the paper. Writing a clear introduction is important as it guides the readers of your paper. For this reason, academics often write their abstract and introduction last.

1. What to include in the introduction

1.1 Background information

It is important to try and gauge the amount of knowledge your audience will have about the topic of your paper. Think about the topic of the paper in the previous chapter on abstracts. When you looked at the title "Happy Material," did you know what it meant? Most of you probably had no clue as to what the paper was about. Thus, in the introduction you need to provide readers with background information about your topic.

Learning Task 1

Read the introduction below from the sample essay "Happy Material" again to see how the author gives readers background information about the topic.

Introduction example 1

> "Happy Material"
>
> "Happy Material," is a song, which was used as an opening song for a TV animation "Magical Teacher Negima." This animation was telecasted in Japan from January 6, 2005 to June 29, 2005. This animation describes a 10-year-old boy who becomes an English teacher at a girls' high school. He takes charge of 3–A. This class has 31 students. "Happy Material" was sung by the students of this class. Although the actual singers were radio actresses, this song was sold in the name of the characters. This song had seven versions. Version 4 ranked third in Oricon hit chart and ranked twentieth in World Single Chart. There are four reasons why "Happy Material" sold well.

1.2 Thesis statement

In addition to the background information about the topic, you need to inform readers about your topic focus in the introduction, which is called a *thesis statement*. In Chapter 6, you briefly learned about thesis statements. You will learn about them more specifically in the following exercise. Before that, here is a review of the characteristics of thesis statements from Chapter 6.

    a. Thesis statements are summaries of your topic focus and help you organize and develop your argument.

b. Good thesis statements:
- are clear and express one main idea;
- are specific to the assignment requirements; and,
- assert your conclusions about a subject.

Based on the description of thesis statements above, what is the thesis statement in the introduction to the student paper "Happy Material"? The answer is the last sentence of the introduction, *There are four reasons why "Happy Material" sold well.* Normally, the thesis statement comes at the end of the introduction. The paper "Happy Material" uses a cause and effect organization. A paper written with this type of organizing structure should focus on a specific result or a phenomenon and analyze reasons for, or causes of, the result. In the sample introduction above, the focused result is good sales of "Happy Material" and the student identified four reasons for that result. This thesis statement serves two important functions. First, from the reader's viewpoint the audience is given an outline of the main points, that is, the four reasons for good sales of "Happy Material." Second, from the writer's perspective the thesis statement helps the author to organize his or her thinking in the rest of the paper; the four reasons need to be discussed in detail in separate paragraphs.

2. Organization of the introduction

The introductory paragraph of an essay "begins by introducing the general idea of the topic and narrows to the specific idea of the thesis statement" (Ruetten, 2003, p. 184). This idea applies to an EGAP paper introduction as well. The general idea of the topic can be background information. Thus, when giving readers background information about your topic, start with a wider, general idea, narrow down the idea, and then finally focus the precise topic of your paper in the thesis statement. This process is expressed as follows:

```
┌─────────────────────────────────────────────┐
│     General Idea/Background Information     │
└─────────────────────────────────────────────┘
                      ↓
         ┌──────────────────────────┐
         │      Specific Idea       │
         └──────────────────────────┘
                      ↓
             ┌──────────────────┐
             │ Thesis Statement │
             └──────────────────┘
```

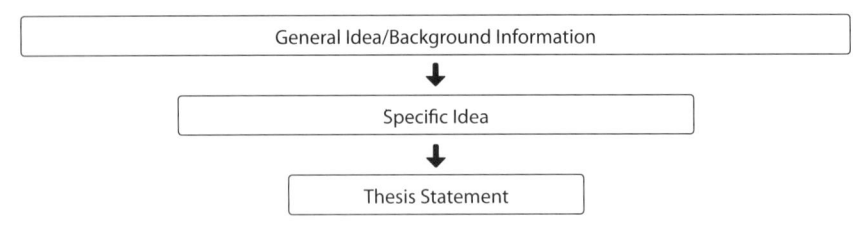

Figure 9.1 General Organization of an Introduction

How does this organizational pattern work in practice? Look at the introduction below from a student paper written using a comparison and contrast organization.

2.1 Sample assignment: comparison and contrast paper

A comparison and contrast organization is one in which the writer analyzes the similarities and differences between two things (see more details of comparison and contrast essays in Chapter 10 and Chapter 13). In the sample assignment here, you will be introduced to the topic of "Western archery and Japanese archery."

Although the pattern **general idea** → **specific idea** → **thesis statement** should be followed in the finished product, it can take time to develop a precise thesis statement.

Step 1: Thesis statement

This assignment is very narrow and simply requires you to discuss either similarities or differences between the two things you choose. Consider Western archery and Japanese archery. On the whole, are they similar or different? In the example here, you conclude that these two types of archery are different, and that becomes your thesis statement.

- Thesis statement: Western and Japanese archery have many differences.

Step 2: Background information

Now you have a focus through your thesis statement, but you need to think about what your audience knows about Western and Japanese archery. Some readers might know them well, but others may not. In fact, some readers might not even understand basic points such as what archery is. To plan an academic paper on this topic for such an audience, you need to answer the following questions:

- What is archery? → It's a sport.
- What do you do in archery? → You try to hit a target.
- What kinds of tools do archers use? → Archers use a bow, arrows, and a target.

Step 3: Specific ideas
Now that you have decided what general information you need to provide readers, you have to determine the specific ideas, or main points, of your paper. To do so, you need to answer the following questions:

- What is your topic? → Western archery and Japanese archery
- What organizational pattern will you use? → Comparison and contrast
- Why did you choose this rhetorical mode for writing? → People may think they are similar, but in fact they are different in many ways. I will focus on the differences.
- What are the key differences? → Decide on these and use them in the body section of your paper.

What you need to do now is put your thoughts in order. Remember that the common organizational pattern of an introduction is from general to specific ideas and ends with a focused thesis statement. Look at the example below.

Introduction example 2

Western Archery and Japanese Archery

Archery is a sport in which anchers use a bow and arrows and aim at a target. People in many countries practice it. There are two types of archery, Western archery and Japanese archery. Many people may assume that they are similar. It is true in some sense. Players fit an arrow to their bow and shoot it toward a target in both of them. However, they actually have many differences.

Although it is short, this is an effective introduction for the assignment. Can you see how the writer moves from general background information, to more specific information and finally to a thesis statement? In the next section, you will practice how to write the introduction for another pattern of organization used in academic writing, argumentation.

2.2 Sample assignment: argumentation paper

Argumentation, or an argumentative academic paper, is a type of writing in which you state your opinion on a given topic, usually take a position, and by making a good argument try to convince readers why the stance you take is correct. Typical topics for argumentative papers include the following:

- Should the university academic year in Japan begin in September?
- Should the age of majority in Japan be lowered to 18 from 20?

Topics for argumentative papers usually involve advantages and disadvantages. The topics tend to be controversial so you must decide whether you are for or against the proposal. Thus, a typical thesis statement for an argumentative paper is as follows:

- Thesis statement: I agree with the proposal to begin the university academic year in Japan in September.

The most important point you have to keep in mind in writing an argumentative paper is that you have to be consistent in your position from the beginning to the end. In other words, if you state that you disagree with the proposal in your thesis statement, you have to be against the proposal throughout your paper and you have to offer convincing reasons why you are against it. For more on the argumentation pattern of organization, see Chapter 10.

Learning Task 2

Use the steps below to write an introduction for an argumentative paper.

Topic: Should business hours of convenience stores be shortened?

Background reading

> 地球温暖化の問題と関連し、京都市は2008年5月、コンビニエンスストアの深夜営業見直しを打ち出し、同年8月には「環境にやさしいライフスタイルを考える市民会議」を始めてこの問題を話し合うことにした。日本フランチャイズチェーン協会は話し合いに参加を求められたがボイコットし、両者は対立関係となった。実際には、コンビニの深夜営業規制に反対する人も多く、規制が実現するかどうかは不透明な状態だ。
> (朝日新聞2008年10月16日 「ニュースがわからん！コンビニ深夜営業規制どうなった？」より要約)

According to the background information above, the proposal for discussion here is that the business hours of convenience stores should be shortened. You must decide whether you agree or disagree with the proposal and provide arguments to support your stance.

Step 1: Thesis statement
Remember from the previous section that the thesis statement often comes at the end of the introduction. Your thesis statement for this paper has to state whether you are for or against the proposal. Remember that in early drafts of academic papers, thesis statements are often "working thesis statements," which means they can change. To get started, circle either *for* or *against* below:

I am for/against the proposal to shorten the late-night business hours of convenience stores.

Step 2: Background information
Now that you have a working thesis statement, you can plan your introduction, using the basic organizational pattern: general idea → specific idea → thesis statement.

In order to follow this pattern for the introduction, you need to read the background information for the topic again and answer the following questions:

a. *Why did Kyoto City propose to shorten the late-night business hours of convenience stores? What are they concerned about?*
   The answer is global warming, a serious problem for all the people on the earth. Thus, general background information on the topic of global warming could be useful.
b. *Regarding efforts to stop global warming, what kinds of measures do you know? Name the measures or groups involved with this issue both at the international level and the country or community level.*

One measure at the international level you can probably think of is the Kyoto Protocol. Could you think of any groups active at the local level? The Kyoto Protocol and the movements in your local community are examples of more specific ideas related to the general topic of global warming.

Step 3: Specific ideas
Now that you have some general ideas about global warming, you need to give more specific background information about the proposal. Read the newspaper article again and answer the following questions:

   a. *What did Kyoto City propose in May 2008?*
   b. *What did Kyoto City form in August 2008?*
   c. *What was the reaction from the Japan Franchise Association?*

Now that you have the answers to these questions, the final step to take is to connect the background information with your thesis statement. A typical ending for an argumentative paper introduction, including the thesis statement, is as follows:
   There are proponents and opponents on this issue, and _____ has / have yet to reach a consensus. In this paper, I will explain why I am for / against the proposal to _____ .

3. Writing an introduction

Background Information: Global warming

⬇

Specific Idea: Measures to stop global warming (international level)
 • Kyoto Protocol
Specific Idea: Measures to stop global warming (local level)
  • Your own examples of the measures at the community level
  • Kyoto City government proposal
  • "Environmentally friendly lifestyles" panel
  • Reaction of Japan Franchise Association

⬇

Ending: There are proponents and opponents concerning this issue. Kyoto City has yet to regulate the business hours of convenience stores. I support / oppose the proposal to shorten the night business hours of convenience stores.

Figure 9.2 Organizing Your Introduction

Learning Task 3

Based on the outline above, write an introduction in your own words.

Title: Should late-night business hours of convenience stores be shortened?

Introduction example 3

Should Late-night Business Hours of Convenience Stores be Shortened?

Global warming is an issue which all countries have to tackle because the rising of the earth's temperature causes enormous problems to people's lives in every part of the globe. While there is a movement at the international level, such as the Kyoto Protocol of 1997, toward moving forward to stop global warming, there are also local movements to encourage people to take actions to stop global warming and save the environment. For example, in Japan, many stores now ask customers to bring their own bags. The stores at Kyoto University in fact do not provide customers with plastic bags for their purchases anymore. In accordance with these local movements in May 2008 Kyoto City proposed to shorten the business hours of convenience stores; the hours from late at night to early morning, in particular. Moreover, in August 2008, Kyoto City formed a panel called "a city council to discuss environmentally-friendly lifestyles." The Japan Franchise Association, which was invited to join the panel, however, refused to participate. Clearly, there are proponents and opponents in regard to this proposal, and Kyoto City has yet to decide to regulate around-the-clock business hours of convenience stores. I am against the proposal to shorten the late-night business hours of convenience stores for several reasons.

4. Revising

Learning Task 4

Read your first draft of an academic paper and decide whether you need to revise your introduction. Then, exchange papers with a classmate and give him/her advice about points that need revision in the introduction.

References

Ruetten, M. K. (2003). *Developing composition skills: Rhetoric and grammar* (2nd ed.). Boston: Thomson & Heinle.

この章のまとめ

introduction 作成の三つのステップは理解できただろうか．読者は必ずしも共通の興味や考えを持っているわけではない．したがって，最初から具体的な問題を提供しては，問題意識が共有できないことがある．読者に問題の背景を伝え，段階的に問題を絞り込んでいかなければならない．問題の共有ができ，論文全体の見取り図があれば，読者は迷うことなく議論に入っていけるだろう．

Chapter 10 Writing the Body Section

> この章のねらい
> いよいよ論文本体の執筆にとりかかる．この章では，特に論文本体の執筆において重要な考え方について学ぶ．論文とは，議論を展開する文章のことである．したがって，論文の執筆においては，議論の展開方法について十分に知っていなければならない．ここでは，文の書き方から始まって，どのようにparagraph（段落）を組み立て，論文本体の構成を行うのかを見ていこう．

The main purpose of the body section of an academic paper is to develop and provide support for the paper's argument, which is first articulated in a *thesis statement* in the introduction (see Chapter 6 and Chapter 9 for more on thesis statements). The body section will almost always be the longest section of an academic paper because much information is necessary to develop the paper's main argument. To write a clear argument, it is essential to carefully organize the body of your paper and use appropriate words that signal transitions between your main points. This may sound simple, but it takes a good deal of practice to master.

This chapter will highlight the following: paragraph structure, basic organization of academic papers, rhetorical modes, and transition signals.

1. Writing paragraphs

Words and sentences are the basic parts of most written human communication. Academic writing demands precision, therefore, it is necessary to practice writing clear sentences that link together in a logical order. This can be one definition of a paragraph.

1.1 Features of paragraphs

In academic writing, paragraphs tend to have three parts:

- A topic sentence
- Supporting sentences that develop the topic
- A concluding sentence

1.1.1 Topic sentences

Topic sentences name the general topic and indicate the limited area of the topic to be discussed in the paragraph. That is, a topic sentence consists of two parts: a general topic and a specific focus. To write the kind of precise descriptions demanded by academic writing you must limit the areas of the topic in your study as a whole, as well as in each body paragraph. As a general rule, a paragraph should be limited to **one main idea or focus.** A topic sentence usually is the first sentence of a paragraph, but can also be positioned last.

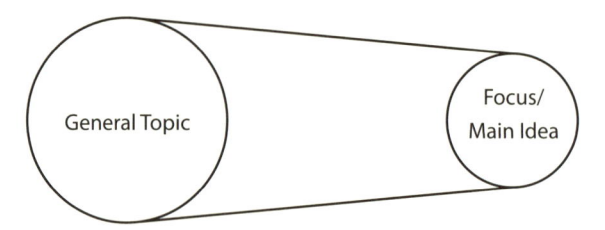

Figure 10.1 Parts of a Topic Sentence

Learning Task 1

Read the three sample topic sentences below. Underline the general topic and circle the main idea focus.

a. University students in Japan who are interested in research foresee roles for themselves in international academic discourse communities.
b. In this context the basic research question takes on a greater meaning: So what?
c. Three groups of people are particularly vulnerable to Internet addiction.

1.1.2 Supporting sentences: Unity and coherence

Once you have identified the general topic and described how you will limit your discussion to a single main idea in the paragraph (focus), you will need to explain and support your main point. The focus is the main idea of the paragraph so the support and details written in the paragraph should be limited to describing that **one main idea only.** Good academic writing depends on *unity* and *coherence*.

Unity means that you write about only one main idea in a paragraph and that the support you use consists of details *directly related* to that main idea.

Learning Task 2

Read the three examples below and decide if the unity of the paragraphs is good or poor.

> Moreover, you must not disturb the privacy of a victim and other persons who are related to the case. And you ought not to reveal another lay judge's name. Of course, you must not make it known that you are a lay judge until judgement is passed on the accused. Do not forget that a lay judge has the duty of confidentiality. A breach of confidentiality is punishable with a fine or prison terms.

Good unity/Poor unity

> Third, there are ethical issues involved. The cloned human has rights as a human, but cloned humans might not be treated as people. In other words, they might be treated more like machines or tools.

Good unity/Poor unity

> Japan must reduce greenhouse gas emissions by 6% of 1990 levels between 2008 and 2012, but these levels are actually rising. Therefore, in Kansai many schools and offices are trying to realize the goal of the Kyoto Protocol. 'Eco bags' are now very popular in Kansai and there is a 'my bag' boom. For example, the stores at Kyoto University no longer offer customers plastic bags for goods.

Good unity/Poor unity

Coherence means that your paragraph is easy to understand. This refers to the logical order of your supporting sentences and your effective use of transition words and phrases.

Learning Task 3

Use transition words and phrases from the short list below to complete the paragraphs.

Transition Signal Words and Phrases		
First(ly),	Next,	Last(ly),
To begin with,	After that,	Most important(ly),
First of all,	Also,	Finally,
	In addition,	
	Second(ly),	

Paragraph 1

> Never look at the sun with the naked eye, through binoculars or a telescope. A safe way to view a solar eclipse is through a pinhole projector. Here is how to make one. _____ you need a long box or tube. _____ cut a hole in the center of one end of the box and tape a piece of foil over the hole. _____ poke a small hole in the foil with a pin. _____ cut a viewing hole in the side of the box. _____ put a piece of white paper inside the end of the box near the viewing portal.

Paragraph 2

> Success in university is not by chance. Good students know how to study effectively. _____ good students practice note taking and take well-organized notes. _____ the best students are involved in their classes and ask questions. _____ top students make learning new vocabulary a high priority. _____ good students do all of their assignments on schedule and read a wide range of materials.

2. Organizing the body

Each paragraph in the body should contain a topic sentence with a main idea that is relevant to the thesis of the paper. A topic sentence, usually at the beginning of each paragraph, should lay the foundation for the paragraph's *unity;* that is, each paragraph should be centered on one single main idea. Besides unity, each paragraph should have *coherence;* in other words, the sentences in each paragraph should flow together logically and smoothly. Finally, a sentence that provides a sense of conclusion to the paragraph's main idea should appear near the end of each paragraph, like the following sentence: *The body section of an academic paper is located between the introduction and the conclusion sections and contains paragraphs with unity and coherence, whose main ideas are linked together to logically develop the paper's thesis.*

2.1 Basic academic paper and paragraph structure

Basic Academic Paper Structure

Introduction

General Information
Paper Outline
Thesis Statement

Body

Main Point 1
a. details-support
b. details-support
c. details-support

Main Point 2
a. details-support
b. details-support
c. details-support

Main Point 3
a. details-support
b. details-support
c. details-support

Conclusion

1. Summarize main ideas
2. Explain importance

Paragraph Structure

Topic Sentence

a. details-support
b. details-support
c. details-support

Concluding Sentence (if needed)

2.2 Rhetorical modes of organization

How should you organize your paper's body section and where does it fit in the context of the entire paper? Be careful not to fall victim to one of the common mistakes made by many beginners of academic writing: *Do not simply collect sections from one or two sources, rearrange the words and then copy them into the body of your paper.* In addition, never copy and paste text directly from Internet sources into your academic paper! This method is very fast, but extremely dangerous and does nothing for your education.

Most university writing assignments demand that you write more than simply your personal opinion about a matter. You should first identify in the introduction an academic issue, problem or research question that is the basis for your argument. Next, in the body section, *explain* theories, *summarize* and *evaluate* evidence, and *analyze* and *synthesize information* (i.e., use information from various sources). Finally, conclude the paper by stating *why* the problem you addressed is significant and relevant, *how* your argument is supported by evidence, *who* will care about this information, and, *what* the important implications are.

A very important consideration is the structure of your paper. Rhetorical patterns of organization are simply different ways of organizing and presenting information. For example, information can be presented in chronological order, that is, organized by time sequence to describe historical events or scientific processes. Categorization or logical division of ideas is another way to organize academic papers. This is simply grouping items according to some quality they have in common.

Three organizational frameworks are outlined in this chapter.

2.2.1 Cause and effect

Use a cause and effect organization when the writing assignment calls for examining the reasons for some phenomenon and the resulting effects of it. Examples of this type of assignment are as follows: explain the high rate of suicide in Japan; and, explain the spread of so-called "super weeds" in modern agriculture. The two methods of structuring cause and effect papers are called *block* organization and *chain* organization.

BLOCK ORGANIZATION	CHAIN ORGANIZATION
(all) Causes	(single) Cause
	↓
(all) Effects	(single) Effect
	(single) Cause
	↓
	(single) Effect

Which pattern should you use? This depends upon the topic you are investigating. If the causes and effects are quite closely related, a chain organization might be best. With broad topics in which direct cause and effect relationships are difficult to determine, the block style organizational pattern is usually easier. However, some topics may require you to combine the block and chain styles of organization.

The main ideas and details that make up paragraphs of a cause and effect pattern paper can be organized in these ways:

- Chronological order: main ideas and details arranged in the order that events occurred
- Order of importance: main ideas and details arranged from most to least important or vice versa
- Categorical order: main ideas and details arranged by dividing the topic into categories

For more on cause and effect organization, see section 3.1.1 below.

2.2.2 Comparison and contrast

Use a comparison and contrast organization when the writing assignment calls for examining similarities and/or differences between things of a similar nature. You can compare and contrast things that are alike (e.g., humans and apes), but you cannot compare and contrast things that are not alike (e.g., viruses and methane gas). Of course, you compare similarities and contrast differences. In fact, the rhetorical modes cause and effect and comparison and contrast have similar patterns of organization. The two patterns for organizing comparison and contrast papers are called *point-by-point* and *block*.

BLOCK ORGANIZATION	POINT-BY-POINT ORGANIZATION
Similarities (or differences) of X and Y a. first point b. second point c. third point Differences (or similarities) between X and Y a. first point b. second point c. third point	Main Point 1 a. X 1. example of X related to main point 1 2. example of X related to main point 1 b. Y 1. example of Y related to main point 1 2. example of Y related to main point 1 Main Point 2 a. X 1. example of X related to main point 2 2. example of X related to main point 2 b. Y 1. example of Y related to main point 2 2. example of Y related to main point 2

When planning your paper, you should choose the style that you think will be easier to write and most effective for the topic. Block style means that you first discuss all of the similarities together in a block (i.e., one paragraph or group of paragraphs) and all of the differences in another block. In the point-by-point pattern, you compare and contrast similarities and differences on each main feature about whatever you are comparing. For more on comparison and contrast organization, see section 3.1.2 below.

2.2.3 Argumentation
Use an argumentation organization when the writing assignment calls for examining the advantages and disadvantages of some proposal. An argumentation

paper normally requires the writer to take a stance and give reasons for their stated opinion. You can approach an argumentation paper as follows:

a. Research the topic (e.g., Should gambling be illegal?)
b. Decide your stance (e.g., Yes, gambling should be illegal.)
c. Define the key terms clearly (e.g., Give your definition of gambling.)
d. Select main ideas from your research that support your stance
e. If your support is weak, do more research and reconsider your main ideas
f. Introduce and refute opposing arguments

Reasoning
There are three types of reasoning:

- Inductive: from a specific point to a more general point
- Deductive: from a general point to a more specific point
- Abductive: identifying a problem and then stating and testing a hypothesis

Evidence
Academic papers normally require that ideas be supported by evidence of some type. Evidence is either extrinsic (data, facts, testimony, authority) or intrinsic (invented). Strong evidence is accurate, representative, and authoritative.

Warrants
Warrants relate to the depth and strength of your argument. They connect your reasons to your main ideas (claims), by relating the evidence for each reason to the claim it supports. They generally fall into one of two categories:
a. A system of commonly held beliefs, based on empirical evidence (e.g., smoke indicates fire)
b. Authority (Because Y is an expert, when he/she says Z, Z must be true.)

To solidify your ideas and write a stronger academic paper, a good practice when using the argument style is to explain some of the opposing main points and refute them. For more on argumentation organization, see section 3.1.3 below.

3. Using transitions

Earlier in this chapter we introduced a few basic transitional words and phrases. These are also called signal words and phrases because they signal important information to readers. Whenever you see a signal word in your reading, you should think that the information that follows it could be important. Transition signals make reading easier in this way. Here, two uses of transitions will be explained. First, some of the transitions linked to the three rhetorical modes are outlined. Following this, examples are shown of how transitions can be used to link paragraphs and make your paper more coherent.

3.1 Transitions linked to specific rhetorical modes

3.1.1 Cause and effect

When writing an academic paper that is organized according to the cause and effect pattern, use transitional words and phrases like these.

Transitions for Signalling Causes	Transitions for Signalling Effects
because	As a result,
due to	Consequently,
One cause is	Thus,
Another cause is	One result is
Since	Therefore,
For that reason,	_____ resulted in _____

3.1.2 Comparison and contrast

When writing an academic paper that is organized according to the comparison and contrast pattern, use transitional words and phrases like these.

Transitions for Signalling Similarities	Transitions for Signalling Differences
Likewise,	however,
Similarly,	nevertheless,
Both X and Y	different from
Neither X nor Y	in contrast
Not only X, but also Y	although
X is similar to Y	while

3.1.3 Argumentation

When writing an academic paper that is organized according to the argumentation pattern, use transitional words and phrases like these.

Transitions for Signalling Your Stance	Transitions for Supporting Your Position
I take the position that	For example,
I believe (that)	For instance,
In my opinion,	To illustrate (my point),

Transitions for Introducing Opposing Arguments	Transitions for Refuting Opposing Arguments
Nevertheless, some people feel	There is a problem with that argument.
Some people disagree with this position	In response, I would point out (that)
On the other hand, some people argue	My response to that argument is

3.2 Linking main ideas between paragraphs

The examples and supporting details in each of your paragraphs need to be joined with transition words and phrases. It is just as important to clearly connect main ideas between paragraphs in the body section.

Learning Task 4

The paragraphs below come from a student essay. Read the paragraphs and choose the correct start for each from the box.

> - To prevent this problem from worsening, or to at least moderate the effects,
> - First of all, increasing the birth rate in Japan seems difficult.
> - In addition, the rising tax burden is only one economic problem caused by the dwindling population.

Topic of this paper: Whether Japan should increase immigration

With Japan's fertility rate now falling way below the replacement rate of 2.1 at 1.22 children born per woman, the country can expect its population to decline by 22 million by 2050 ("Japan Total Fertility Rate," 2008). To make up for this decrease in population, allowing more immigration is an option for the Japanese government to consider.

_____ However, increasing the inflow of foreigners in the country can help to increase the population in a short span of time. This will widen Japan's tax base, thus relieving the growing tax burden on Japanese workers.

_____ With a smaller workforce, the current economic level will become unsustainable in time. In other words, a labor shortage will result in a slowdown of Japan's economy. Already, many Japanese companies are forced to hire temporary foreign workers (McNicol, 2008). Many of the jobs taken by unskilled foreign laborers are difficult and dangerous.

_____ Japan can either take active steps to increase the birth rate, or allow more immigration. As mentioned above, increasing the birth rate is not as easy as it may seem. Not only that, but the effects of an increase in the birth rate can

> only be seen after a period of 15 years or so. Opening up immigration, on the other hand, can lead to more immediate population and labor relief.

It is important to think of your academic paper **as a whole.** Your paper is a unit that is framed by the thesis statement and the introduction. Next, come the main ideas that relate to the focus in your thesis statement. Each main idea should be connected by using good transitions in your paragraphs. Transitional words and phrases are basic, simple words, but they have a lot of power to make your writing more understandable. Do not forget to use them!

4. Revising

Learning Task 5

Read your first draft of an academic paper and decide what you need to revise. Then, exchange papers with a classmate and give him/her advice about areas to revise.

My draft paper		My classmate's draft paper	
•PARAGRAPHS: ☐good ☐revise		•PARAGRAPHS: ☐good ☐revise	
Specific problems:	☐topic sentences ☐unity ☐coherence	Specific problems:	☐topic sentences ☐unity ☐coherence
•ORGANIZATION: ☐good ☐revise		•ORGANIZATION: ☐good ☐revise	
Specific problems:	☐rhetorical mode ☐not logical ☐more/better transitions	Specific problems:	☐rhetorical mode ☐not logical ☐more/better transitions
•CONTENT: ☐good ☐revise		•CONTENT: ☐good ☐revise	
Specific problems:	☐few sources ☐poor sources ☐weak main points ☐poor examples/details	Specific problems:	☐few sources ☐poor sources ☐weak main points ☐poor examples/details

For more detailed exercises on peer advice, see Chapter 14.

この章のまとめ

論文本体における議論の展開方法について理解できただろうか．「cause and effect（原因と結果）」や「comparison and contrast（比較と対比）」といった考え方や，自分の意見や立場の提示とその意見や立場を支える例の提示といった典型的な議論の展開方法は，論文作成する際，常に意識しておいてほしい．また，論文においては，段落という形式はルールに基づいて構成されていなければならない．文から段落へ，段落から節へというように部分から全体へ構成していくことによって，議論をより強固なものにすることができるだろう．

Chapter 11 Writing the Conclusion

> この章のねらい
> 論文には結論が必要である．論文本体の途中で，議論の結論は出ているから必要ないだろうと思ってはいけない．結論には，議論の結果を確認するという重要な役割がある．さらに，ある議論が一つの論文だけで完結することはまずありえない．ほとんどの論文は新しい問題を生み，次の研究や論文へとつながっていく．論文のconclusion（結論）には，そのような役割もある．適切なconclusionの書き方について見ていこう．

The conclusion is important because it is the last thing people read in your paper. Therefore, it is what they are most likely to remember after they've finished the paper. The conclusion is the end of a paper, but you shouldn't write The End like in a movie. Also, an ending such as that's all is too abrupt. While it is true that the conclusion marks the end of your paper, it need not be the end of the discussion. If possible, try to leave the readers of your paper with something interesting to think about after they finish reading your paper.

This chapter will discuss the contents of a conclusion and present some examples from student research papers.

1. Writing an effective conclusion

> **Three Basic Conclusion Styles**
>
> 1. Summarize the thesis statement and main points
> 2. Explain why the information in the paper is important
> 3. Add to the outline of the topic explained in the introduction

Learning Task 1

Read the introductions, body summaries and conclusions below. Decide which conclusion style is being used (1, 2, or 3).

Topic: Japan's immigration policy

Introduction

The population of Japan is now declining. According to the 2008 white paper on the declining birthrate, the Japanese population will decrease from 127.7 million in 2005 to 89.9 million in 2055. This means that there will not be enough workers to support the nation. In this paper, I will consider one possible solution, opening Japan to foreign immigration. This policy change has a number of advantages and disadvantages.

Body Main Points

Advantages:
- do unwanted jobs
- do vital jobs (e.g., nursing)

Disadvantages:
- unable to adjust to Japan
- become a burden on the state

Conclusion

The importance of this issue for Japan should be clear. Because the population is decreasing, it is obvious that Japan will need more workers in various fields. This labour shortage is probably the most important factor. Of course, some immigrants might have trouble adjusting to life in Japan and that is why government programs will be important. To succeed in accepting immigrants, it is essential that we work with them and try to encourage them to adjust to Japanese society.

Conclusion style: _____

Topic: Climate change

Introduction

Today the earth is facing great difficulties related to food, population and the environment. People are especially concerned with abnormal weather because it concerns the lives of people all over the world. My position is that the situation with regard to climate change is becoming critical for human civilization. In this essay, I will argue that climate destruction is largely anthropocentric and must be checked. I will then provide a basic outline of the Kyoto Protocol of 1997 and describe how institutions in the Kansai region of Japan are taking action in support of the protocol.

Body Main Points

Outline of 1997 Kyoto Protocol
Actions in Kansai Area
- Eco bags
- suggestion: greening cities through better traffic control

Conclusion

Many scientists say that the present situation is very serious. They claim that if we do not change climate destruction will continue as the surface temperature will rise from 4 to 6°C (Flannery, 2006). This means that humans need to do more to change the situation. The government of Japan now pledges that by 2020 the country will cut greenhouse emissions by 15% of the 2005 level. Given the seriousness of the current situation, this seems to be too little, too late. The Japanese people can do better. This is an issue that Japan should lead the world on.

Conclusion style: _____

Topic: Food trade and security

Introduction

Today, there is abundant food around us which we take for granted. Most people who shop at supermarkets do not consider how or where food they buy was produced. Japan imports a wide variety of food so that a lot of food in our refrigerators were not produced in Japan. According to the Ministry of Agriculture, Forestry and Fisheries (2008), Japan's food production self sufficiency is around 40%.

In fact, since food is so plentiful, most people are unaware that food trade is closely related to environmental and security issues. The purpose of this essay is to reveal problems with food trade and the relationship of that trade with the environment and security.

Body Main Points

Water Shortages and Food Trade
- concept of "virtual water"
- Japan imports water through wheat and beef imports

WTO Doha Round and Food Trade
- tariffs for Japanese agriculture
- failure of Doha Round

Conclusion

This paper showed how the food trading system carries with it truly serious problems for Japan. Because Japan has one of the lowest food self-sufficiency rates among the OECD nations, it imports a lot of water from developing countries. This water cannot be used by these countries for growing their own food. On the other hand, Japan protects agricultural products like rice that other countries produce much cheaper. This causes conflict internationally and led to the failure of the World Trade Organization (WTO) talks at Doha. In these ways and more, food trade is deeply connected to current problems with the environment and security.

Conclusion style: _____

Learning Task 2

Which of these three styles do you think is the best? Why?

2. Write a conclusion

Learning Task 3

Look at your paper draft with a classmate and discuss these questions together. Do you have a conclusion? Is it a well-written conclusion? Which style of conclusion did you write? How can you improve your conclusion?

Learning Task 4

Make an outline of the main points in your paper. Choose a conclusion style and write a conclusion for your academic paper.

Topic: _____

Conclusion style: _____

Introduction — Write the thesis statement here:

Body Main Points — List the main points of your paper here:

Conclusion

3. Peer advice

Learning Task 5

Ask different classmates to read your new conclusion. What is their opinion of your work? Do they have suggestions to help you improve your conclusion?

4. Weak conclusions

Here are three of the most common weak conclusion styles. Be careful not to use them in your papers.

4.1 The mirror image

This is the most common type of weak conclusion. In this style, the writer repeats the thesis statement and summarizes the main ideas using almost exactly the same language. Be sure to vary your language and expand your ideas when writing a conclusion.

4.2 The waste basket

This type of conclusion includes many new main ideas and/or details that were not included in the body of the paper. Be sure to write your main ideas in the body and explain them well with clear details and examples. Do not cram your conclusion with a lot of new information.

4.3 The wild surmise

From the word wild you might guess that this type of conclusion "jumps to conclusions." What does that mean? It means that you over-generalize and your conclusion makes statements that are too broad without evidence to support the claims. For example,

Human cloning will lead mankind to certain disaster in the future.

Be careful about making absolute statements that use words like *certain, absolutely, all, always, surely, without doubt* and so forth. To avoid overgeneralization, use words like: *some, a number of, many, likely to, may, might, possibly, could,* and *often*.

5. Longer conclusion sample

Conclusions can be longer than just one or two paragraphs. Here is an example written by a Kyoto University undergraduate student. Read it and reflect on the conclusion you have written for your paper.

Topic: The lay judge system in Japan

Conclusion

As stated before, the present lay judge system has too many institutional defects to bring it into operation. Because of this system, a lot of white-collar workers may be subjected to a financial disadvantage, some lay judges may feel distress and be exposed to danger, and the supreme law of Japan may be ignored. But the government has put these questions on the side. This is such a gross blunder that we should not look over it.

However, it is true that this system will be beneficial to the state if it works well; the point is how this system should be made better. I think there are four things that should be done. First, companies should give lay judges a suitable environment. Hiroshi Mori (2008) rightly points out that it is a good idea to create a *saiban-in kyūka* system. This is a system in which a company grants an employee who takes part in a trial as a lay judge a kind of leave of absence. Introducing this system is making progress among large enterprises, including Toyota, Canon and Mandom. As the number of the staff is limited, it may be difficult for small and medium enterprises to bring in the system. But they should immediately consider whether it will be introduced.

Secondly, the government and the Supreme Court should improve the system of protecting lay judges. To be concrete, lay judges should be permitted to screen their face; otherwise their daily lives will entail a constant element of danger. Also it is necessary to provide thorough after-care for lay judges when their role has completed. According to an article of The *Yomiuri Shimbun* (2009), the Supreme Court has provided a service by which a lay judge and a former lay judge can receive counseling free up to five times. However, will five sessions of counseling be enough? To begin with, why is the lay judge system applied to a serious affair? It is important not only to make lay judges feel better after a trial is over but also to prevent them from sustaining an emotional injury.

Thirdly, the lay judge system should be checked against the Constitution of Japan. It is not as if I believe that this system should be annulled because it is against the supreme law. But I think that it is wrong of even the Supreme Court to ignore the view that the lay judge system is against the Constitution. If the Court does not think that the lay judge system is unconstitutional, the Court should explain the reason for it. If the Court recognises that this system is in breach of the Constitution, however, the Court should immediately suspend the system and create a new system that is adapted to it. This should be done, because the Supreme Court is called "the guardian of the Constitution."

Fourthly, there should be a chance that the lay judge system will be improved. Before the lay judge system began to be enforced, many mock trials were conducted. An article of *The Nishi-nippon Shimbun* (2007) points out that there a professional judge often led lay judges to arrive at a certain conclusion. Even though they do not intend to do so, lay judges might bend to professional judges' opinions because they have no judging experience. If such a thing occurs in a real trial, however, we cannot declare it openly. If we do, we will be punished. This is a potentially serious problem. The way in which professional judges should take part in trials should be considered more carefully.

However, the most important thing for us to understand is what the lay judge system is. In other words, we should understand both its strong and weak points in order to improve this system. If so, the lay judge system can be improved.

───── **この章のまとめ**

conclusion は論文の最後でもあり，新しい議論の始まりでもある．論文はただ終わればよいというものではなく，論文が終わった後にも読者に問題を提供し続けるものである．論文本体の作成で力尽きて本文を繰り返したり，論文の議論から大きく離れた結論を述べたりしないように気をつけよう．

Chapter 12
Citing Sources and Writing the References Section

この章のねらい

これまで見てきたように，学術論文では議論に使用した情報を必ず明らかにしなければならない．情報の多くは参考文献という形で表すことになるが，これらはただ示せばよいわけではない．ここでは，適切な参考文献の示し方について見ていく．さらに，参考文献の情報を参照する場合には，適切な方法に従った citation（引用）を行わなければならない．学術論文における citation の方法についても見ていこう．

As you know from Chapter 7, when you write an academic paper, it is important to acknowledge sources of information not only to give credit to the source, but also to inform the reader of details about the original source material. The practice of acknowledging sources is one of the features that distinguish academic writing from non-academic writing, and this practice is called *citation*. To cite is the act of acknowledging sources of information. Exactly when should you cite sources and what is a proper way to do this? This chapter aims to answer these questions and provides opportunities for you to practice writing your own citations for your academic paper.

1. Citing sources of information

1.1 When to cite sources

You must cite sources in your paper when you do the following:

- Use the same words exactly as published in an original source
- Paraphrase or summarize material in a source
- Write about ideas or facts that are not common knowledge
- Report statistics or results from a research paper

1.2 How to cite sources

Every time you do one of the above, you also need to do two things:

- Firstly, identify the source of information you are referring to in the text of your paper (using in-text citations).
- Secondly, list essential information that is necessary to identify the source in a references section at the end of your paper (using reference citations), so that anyone reading your paper could find the information if they wished to look for it.

2. In-text citations

The way to note the source of the material that you refer to in the text of your paper is by using *in-text citations*. In-text citations include the following information:

a. author's family name
b. year of the publication
c. exact page numbers of the source (this is only necessary for quotations)

There are two ways to write an in-text citation:

1) Write the family name of the author in a sentence and put the year of the publication (and page numbers for quotations) in parentheses:

According to Johns (1997), all academic written texts share several characteristics.

2) After using information from a source, put both the family name of the author and the year of the publication (and page numbers for quotations) in parentheses:

Each genre has its own unique "content structure or format, style, and various conventions" (Jordan, 1997, p. 166).

3. The reference list

In-text citations are citations found in the text of your paper. Another type of citation is found in a list at the end of the text of an academic paper. This is called a *reference citation*. In fact, each in-text citation should correspond to a reference citation that is listed at the end of your academic paper. With these two pieces of information, the reader can know the sources of information used in the paper, and is also able to locate and read these source of information for an independent evaluation of the text you are citing.

In the case of the in-text citation examples above, the corresponding reference citations are the following (check the reference list of Chapter 1 to find them yourself):

> Johns, A. (1997). *Text, role and context: Developing academic literacies.* Cambridge: Cambridge University Press.

> Jordan, R. R. (1997). *English for academic purposes: A guide and resource book for teachers.* Cambridge: Cambridge University Press.

4. Advanced points about citation

4.1 How to use "as cited in"

If you do not have the original material, but find a good source that is cited in another source, what should you do?

Most of your professors would probably recommend that you consult the references list in the secondary source, find the material, and read the primary source of information. By reading the original material yourself, you can directly cite the primary source. But sometimes this is not possible. In this case, you should use the following in-text citation format:

(author of the primary source, year, as cited in author of the secondary source, year)

In the following example of a paraphrase, the writer is citing information in a book called *The Altruism Question,* and he cites a particular research study that is cited in the book, by using "as cited in" in the in-text citation:

The feeling of empathy, in turn, leads to an ultimate concern for the needy person's welfare and "pure" altruism is the result, according to the empathy-altruism hypothesis (Batson et al., 1981, as cited in Batson, 1991).

4.2 A Note on et al.

In the in-text citation above the marker *et al.* is used. As you do academic research, eventually you will see the abbreviation et al. used in in-text citations. What does et al. mean? Et al. is an abbreviation from the Latin language that means "and others." Generally speaking, et al. is used in in-text citations when there are over three authors for a source of information. So, in the example above, the meaning is Batson and others (i.e., Batson's colleagues).

Learning Task 1

There are other important abbreviations used in this book. Try to find out the meaning of these three: e.g., i.e., and cf.

Here is the reference list citation corresponding to the in-text citation above (notice that only a reference to the **secondary source** is needed):

Batson, C. D. (1991). *The altruism question: Toward a social psychological answer.* Hillsdale, NJ: Lawrence Erlbaum Associates.

4.3 APA citation guidelines

There are several different referencing guidelines used in academic writing. One standard set of guidelines that is used widely by academics particularly in the social science disciplines is the American Psychological Association (APA) style. The following is a summary of some of the guidelines for source documentation in the APA style. Following this brief summary are some learning tasks to help you become familiar with source documentation using in-text citations and reference citations.

Learning Task 2

Look at the APA source documentation guidelines below. Follow this guide and make a reference list for your academic paper. Be sure to do the following:

- Arrange your reference citations in alphabetical order according to the authors' family names,
- include the date of publication in brackets,
- put the title of the book or journal into *italicized* text, and
- pay attention to punctuation and other minor details.

5. Highlights of the American Psychological Association (APA) source documentation guidelines[1]

The following are examples of the types of references you might use for your research paper. Please note that there are many more specific guidelines for other kinds of sources not listed here. Consult the following resources for more information:

American Psychological Association. (2010). *Publication Manual of the American Psychological Association* (6th ed.). Washington, DC: Author.

The APA Web site: http://www.apastyle.org/manual/index.aspx

1. Books
1.1 Book By A Single Author
1.2 Book By Multiple Authors
1.3 Edited Book
1.4 Chapter In An Edited Book
1.5 Non-English Book

2. Periodicals
2.1 Journal Article
2.2 Magazine Article
2.3 Newspaper Article
2.4 Classroom Handout
2.5 TV Program/DVD

3. Electronic material & lecture notes
- 3.1 Internet Source In-text Citation
- 3.2 Online Journal Article
- 3.3 Online Newspaper Article
- 3.4 Lecture Notes, Including Powerpoint (In-text Citation Only)

1. Books

1.1 Book by a single author
Family name, Initial. (year). *Title of book*. Publication location: Publisher.

Pennycook, A. (1994). *The cultural politics of English as an international language*. London: Longman.

1.2 Book by multiple authors
Family name, Initial., & Family name, Initial. (year). *Title of book*. Publication location: Publisher.

Rubin, J., & Thompson, I. (1994). *How to be a more successful language learner*. Boston: Heinle & Heinle.

1.3 Edited book
Family name, Initial. (Ed.). (year). *Title of book*. Publication location: Publisher.

Stewart, T. (Ed.). (2009). *Insights on teaching speaking in TESOL*. Alexandria, VA: Teachers of English to Speakers of Other Languages, Inc.

1.4 Chapter in an edited book
Chapter author's family name, Initial. (year). Title of chapter. In + Initial and editor's family name (Ed.), *Title of book* (chapter pages). Publication location: Publisher.

Rosenfeld, P., Landis, D., & Dalsky, D. (2003). Evaluating diversity programs. In J. E. Edwards, J. C. Scott, & N. S. Raju (Eds.), *The human resources program-evaluation handbook* (pp. 343–362). Thousand Oaks, CA: Sage.

1.5 Non-English book
Family name, Initial. (year). *Title of book in original language* [Translated title of book]. Publication location: Publisher.

Uzawa, H. (1998). *Nihon no kyôiku wo kangaeru* [Thinking about Japanese education]. Tokyo: Iwanami Shoten.

2. Periodicals

2.1 Journal article
Family name, Initial. (year). Title of article. *Name of Journal, volume*(number), pages.

Chen, H., & Graves, M. F. (1995). Effects of previewing and providing background knowledge on Taiwanese college students: Comprehension of American short stories. *TESOL Quarterly, 29*(4), 385–388.
Hadley, G. S. (1999). Innovative curricula in tertiary ELT: A Japanese case study. *ELT Journal, 53*(1), 92–99.

2.2 Magazine article
Family name, Initial. (year, Month). Title of article. *Name of Magazine, volume,* pages.

Hochman, P. (1998, April). Posting up the NBA. *Dunk Shoot, 63,* 100–101.
Title of article. (year, Month). *Name of Magazine,* pages.
- Use if there is no author.
- Cite the title in "quotation marks," and year in the in-text citation.

Lawsuit challenging Sprewell suspension dismissed again. (1999, May). *Sports Illustrated, 25.*

2.3 Newspaper article
Family name, Initial. (year, Month day). Title of article. *Name of Newspaper,* page.
Title of article. (year, Month day). Name of Newspaper, pages.
- Use if there is no author.

- Cite the title in "quotation marks," and year in the in-text citation.

Fukukawa, S. (1999, July 6). Education system still far too rigid. *The Daily Yomiuri,* p. 6.

Education in crisis. (2009, July 16). *The Asahi Shimbun,* p. 9.

2.4 Classroom Handout

Family name, Initial. (year, Month). *Title of handout.* Handout presented in Name and Location of Course.

Thompson, S. (1997, May) *Asian women in country music.* Handout presented in Introduction to Sociology at Miyazaki International College, Miyazaki, Japan.

2.5 TV program/DVD

Creator's family name, Initial. (Job Title). (year, Month day). *Title of program.* Location of broadcasting company: Broadcasting company.

Creator's family name, Initial. (Job Title). (year). *Title of program.* [Type of Media]. (Available from location: name of distribution company).

Byrnes, J. (Producer). (2000, July 30). *Rice terraces in the Philippines.* Tokyo: TBS.

Cran, W. (Producer). (1986). [DVD]. (Available from Chicago, IL: Public Media Incorporated).

3. Electronic material & lecture notes

3.1 In-text citation

- If you know the author use the standard format (Author, year). If there is no author, quote the title of the article ("title," year). Use n.d. if there is no date.

3.2 Online journal article

Family name, Initial. (year). Title of article. *Title of Journal, volume*(number), page. doi:
- doi = digital object identifier

Wheeler, G. (2009). Plagiarism in the Japanese universities: Truly a cultural matter? *Journal of Second Language Writing, 18*(1), 17–29. doi: 10.1016/j.jslw.2008.09.004

Family name, Initial. (year). Title of article. *Title of Journal, volume*(number), page. Retrieved from: URL
- Use this style if there is no doi

Leu, D. J., Jr. (2000). Our children's future: Changing the focus of literacy and literacy instruction. *Reading Online, 53,* 424–431. Retrieved from: http://www.readingonline.org/electronic/RT/focus/

3.3 Online newspaper article
Family name, Initial. (year, Month). Title of article. *Name of Newspaper,* page. Retrieved from: URL

Takeuchi, T. (1999, November). Schools getting a head start on English curriculum. *APA Monitor,* 1–3. Retrieved from: http://www.yomiuri.co.jp/newse/1122cu15.htm

3.4 Lecture notes, including PowerPoint slides (in-text citation only)
Lecture notes are considered to be a personal communication so a reference citation is not necessary; however, spoken words from a lecture should be noted in an in-text citation as follows:

In an Educational Linguistics lecture, Professor Tajino said …

…(A. Tajino, Educational Linguistics lecture, May 20, 2009).
- Use quotation marks if it is an exact quote

6. Using the APA referencing style

6.1 Non-English materials

Learning Task 3

Put the information below into the correct APA reference citation format for an academic paper written in English.

宇宙への秘密の鍵 (単行本)
スティーヴン ホーキング (著)，ルーシー ホーキング (著)
岩崎書店，東京
2008

6.2 Listing materials in alphabetical order

Learning Task 4

Put the names in the left column into the correct APA format (i.e., family name and initial) and list them in the right column in the proper alphabetical order.

Mayumi Fujioka	
Tim Stewart	
Akira Tajino	
Craig Smith	
David Dalsky	
Barack Obama	
Leo van Lier	
Toshiyuki Kanamaru	
Sayako Maswana	

6.3 Listing materials in the reference list

Examine the information below about two sources of information.

In-text Citation 1
According to Wallace (2002, p. 111), "A key factor in the students' progress to critique and creativity by way of literate English is their ability and willingness to resist."

In-text Citation 2
Qualitative research is being used today in many academic fields (Holliday, 2002).

Text 1 Information
  Chapter Title: Local literacies and global literacy
  Book Title: Globalization and language teaching
  Book Editors: David Block and Deborah Cameron
  Chapter Author: Catherine Wallace
  Page Numbers: 101–114
  Place of Publication: London
  Year of Publication: 2002
  Publisher: Routledge

Text 2 Information
  Book Title: Doing and writing qualitative research
  Book Author: Adrian Holliday
  Place of Publication: Thousand Oaks, CA
  Year of Publication: 2002
  Publisher: Sage Publications

Learning Task 5

Look at the information for these two texts again and use it to write the reference list citation in the APA style.

Reference Citation (in the reference list at the end of your paper)

6.4 Revising an APA reference citation list

Learning Task 6

There are several errors in the reference list below, including missing information. Circle the errors in this reference list and then compare your findings with a partner. Next, on a separate piece of paper, rewrite the reference list correctly.

References

Sandholtz, J. H. (2000). Interdisciplinary team teaching as a form of professional development. *Teacher Education Quarterly, 27*(3), pp. 39–54.

Katsura, H., & Matsune, M. 1994. Team teaching in university conversation courses. In M. Wada & A. Cominos (Eds.), *Studies in team teaching* (pp. 178–185). Kenkyusha.

Dudley-Evans, T. (2001). Team-teaching in EAP: Changes and adaptations in the Birmingham approach. In J. Flowerdew & M. Peacock (eds.), *Research perspectives on English for academic purposes* (pp. 225–238). Cambridge University Press: Cambridge.

Davis, J. R. (1995). *Interdisciplinary Courses and Team Teaching*. Washington, DC: Oryx Press.

Ambler, L. (2007, Fall). *The people decide: The effect of the introduction of the quasi-jury system (Saiban-In Seido) on the death penalty in Japan*. Retrieved from http://www.law.northwestern.edu/journals/JIHR/v6/n1/1/

Kigyou no Saiban-in Kyūka Seido. The Yomiuri Shimbun [Newspaper, selected stories on-line]. Retrieved from http://www.yomiuri.co.jp/atmoney/trend/dr/20090210-OYT8T00619.htm

7. Checking your citations

To repeat one last time, you must support main ideas in an academic paper with evidence. If you have read something useful for your paper in a secondary or primary source, be sure to cite it both with an in-text citation and a full citation in the reference list.

Learning Task 7

First, read your paper and underline all of the most important supporting evidence you give for your main points. Do you have in-text citations for this information? Second, check that your in-text citations and reference citations match. All of the sources in your reference list should be noted in in-text citations as well.

Note

1   Adapted from material prepared by Bill Perry and Katharine Isbell.

この章のまとめ

学術論文における citation の方法には，実に多くの方法，形式があることが分かっただろうか．また，適切な方法を身につけておかなければ，どんなに優れた論文であっても，受け入れてはもらえないことを覚えておこう．ここでは代表的な形式である APA スタイルを例に見ていったが，実際に論文を投稿する場合には，投稿先の学会や論文誌の規定に従わなければならない．論文を作成する前に，必ず参考文献の citation の形式について調べておくようにしよう．

Part III
Academic Writing Classes at Kyoto University

Introduction to
Part III

　パートIIIは，先の二つのパートとはやや傾向が異なり，アカデミックライティング授業の実践紹介である．ここでは京都大学の全学共通教育課程で行われている，アカデミックライティングの三つのクラスを紹介する．

　13章では，パートIIの9章や10章で学んだ論文を構成する文章の構造についての授業紹介が中心となる．特に「比較と対比」についての考え方を学ぶ（教える）には，どのように進めていけばよいかの参考になるだろう．14章はライティング内容の評価，特に学生同士のピアレビューを中心とした授業の紹介である．具体的な例題を提示しているので，実際に活用してみることをお勧めする．最後の15章は，アカデミックライティングにCALL授業を取り入れたハイブリッド授業の紹介である．現在，学術論文のほとんどはコンピュータの使用が前提となっており，ICT技術の活用やその使用方法を学ぶことも必須となりつつある．参考となるウェブサイトも紹介しているので，自身の環境で確認してみてはいかがだろうか．

　ここで紹介するアカデミックライティングの授業は京都大学で行われている授業のごく一部である．京都大学では，週に250コマを越える共通教育の英語が行われており，その4割弱がアカデミックライティングの授業である．一般にライティングの授業は難しいとされるが，ここでの実践例はアカデミックライティング技能の向上に，教育の側が何を提供できるかを示している．

Chapter 13

Focusing on Structure: Comparison and Contrast

In this chapter parts of lessons from academic writing classes at Kyoto University are introduced with samples of writing that students produced.

In Part I of this book you learned that there are certain structural elements of a research paper (e.g., abstract, introduction, body, conclusion, reference list, and some specific moves in the introduction). Moreover, in Part II, you learned step-by-step procedures to write an academic paper. Here, you will learn how to produce one type of EGAP paper with a specific structure: a comparison and contrast paper.

1. Guidelines for writing a comparison/contrast paper

As briefly introduced in Chapter 9 and Chapter 10, the rhetorical mode of comparison/contrast deals with similarities or differences. If you are mainly concerned with the similarities, this is *comparing*. If you focus on the differences, this is *contrasting*.

1.1 Brainstorm and research

Select two things or two people that you want to compare or contrast. The important thing to remember here is that you should select two that are comparable. For example, you cannot compare an apple and a lion; they are from two different categories. Think about some categories, such as sports, food, animals, tools and instruments, and then select two things from the same category. Here are some examples of topics previously generated by students:

- soccer and futsal
- waltz and rumba
- Western archery and Japanese archery

- soba and udon
- Earth and Mars
- Linux and Windows
- University of Tokyo and Kyoto University
- Osaka and Yokohama

When you have selected your topic, you should search for information. Although you may already have some knowledge about the topic you choose, your knowledge might be limited. You can research information from various sources, including books, the Internet, encyclopedias, or even interviewing people who know your topic well (see Chapter 7).

When you finish your research, write down the similarities and differences between the two subjects. To help your understanding, filling in the Venn diagram below might be helpful (adopted from Folse, Muchmore-Vokoun, & Solomon, 2004):

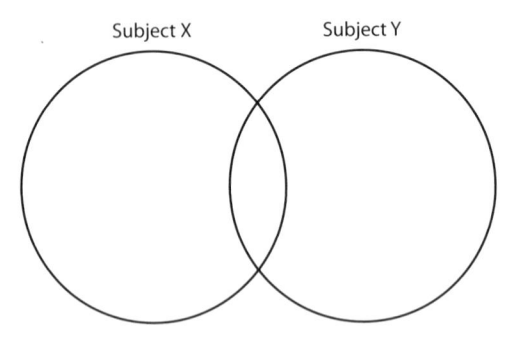

Figure 13.1 Venn Diagram

1.2 Review important phrases

Before putting your ideas into writing, you need to review transition signal words and phrases (see Chapter 10). Below are examples of key signal words and phrases.

a) To show similarities:
Likewise, similarly, also, like, just as, similar to, the same as, both A and B, neither A nor B

Examples
- New York City is the center of economy, culture, and fashion of the U.S. *Likewise,* Tokyo is the center of economic and cultural activities of Japan.
- *Both* Kyoto *and* Nara were the capital of Japan at one time in Japanese history.

b) To show differences:
In contrast, on the other hand, however, while, whereas, although, though, but, yet, unlike, different from

Examples
- Japanese tend to say *"Sumimasen* (I'm sorry)*"* even though they are not responsible for the fault. *In contrast,* Americans usually say "I'm sorry" only when they acknowledge their faults.
- *Different from* Korean women who do not change their family names after marriage, most Japanese women change their family names to their husbands' when they marry.

Signal words and phrases are very important. As you write your paper, carefully choose the best ones to make your ideas clear.

1.3 Choose an organizational pattern

Although there are different organizational patterns for a comparison/contrast paper, here you are introduced to a pattern called the *point-by-point method,* in which the writer presents "both subjects under one point of comparison before moving on to the next point" (Folse, Muchmore-Vokoun, & Solomon, 2004, p. 64). Here is an example of the point-by-point paper outline. The topic is a comparison of the social behavior of Russians and Americans (slightly modified from Folse et al., p. 65, 2004).

Introduction	Paragraph 1	Background information Thesis statement
Body	Paragraph 2	At parties •Russian social behavior •American social behavior
	Paragraph 3	In school •Russian social behavior •American social behavior
	Paragraph 4	At home •Russian social behavior •American social behavior
Conclusion	Paragraph 5	Restated thesis statement Informed opinion

1.4 Write a thesis statement

Before writing an outline or draft of your paper, first you should answer the following questions:

- What are you comparing or contrasting?
- Are you going to focus on the similarities or differences?

After you decide on your topic and focus, write a tentative thesis statement. Here are typical sentences that work as a thesis statement for a comparison/contrast paper (from Huizenga, Snellings, & Francis, 1997, p. 81):

- X and Y *have many things in common.*
- X and Y *have few things in common.*
- X and Y *are very similar.*
- X and Y *are very different.*
- X and Y *share many similarities.*
- X and Y *have many differences.*
- X *resembles* Y.
- X and Y *differ.*
- X is *similar to* Y.
- X *is different from* Y.

1.5 Write an outline

After you write your thesis statement, you should focus on at least three points of either similarities or differences between the two subjects. Then, make an outline based on the point-by-point-method introduced earlier.

1.6 Write a draft

Introduction
Recall the organizational pattern of the introduction from a general to a specific idea and finally to the thesis statement (see Chapter 9).

General idea → Specific idea → Thesis statement

As discussed previously, a general idea can be background information. Since you are comparing or contrasting two subjects (X and Y), you can start with the large category to which X and Y belong. Then, if you are going to focus on the similarities, you may introduce differences between them. In contrast, if you are going to focus on the differences, you may introduce similarities that X and Y share. Finally, in your thesis statement, you can claim one of the following:

- Although X and Y seem to be different, they share many similarities.
- Although X and Y share some similarities, they are different in many ways.

Here are two examples of first-draft introductions.

Example 1:

> Regulation-ball tennis and softball tennis
>
> Tennis is one of the most popular sports in the world. Tennis began in France in the 8th century. At first, people hit a ball with their hands. In Japan, in addition to regulation-ball tennis, a lot of people enjoy softball tennis. We enjoy regulation-ball tennis and softball tennis with a racket and a ball. Therefore, it seems that regulation-ball tennis and softball tennis are very similar. However, there are many differences between regulation-ball tennis and softball tennis.

Example 2:

> Waltz and Rumba
>
> Ballroom dance has formally ten different dance styles. Among these ten styles, waltz and rumba are two of the most well-known styles. However, as most people have only a vague idea about ballroom dance, they often think that these two dances are quite similar. This is true to some extent; both the waltz and the rumba use slow music, and therefore are relatively easy to learn for beginners. Yet they are quite different in many points.

In both of the examples above, the authors provide enough background information for the readers about their topics. In addition, they both give specific information about the similarities between the two subjects, and finally make an effective thesis statement in claiming that despite those similarities, the two subjects are quite different.

Body
For the outline, you were asked to select three points of either similarities or differences between the two subjects you chose. Now you need to develop the discussion of these three points and make them into three separate paragraphs. These three paragraphs together make the body section. At the beginning of each of the three paragraphs, you need a topic sentence in which you specify the point of comparison. There are typical topic sentence patterns for either comparing or contrasting. Some examples are:

(For comparing)
- First, both X and Y are …
- Second, X and Y are similar to each other in …
- Finally, X and Y share similarities in …

(For contrasting)
- One major difference is …
- Another difference is …
- Finally, X and Y are different in …

After each topic sentence, you should give detailed information about the point of the comparison and tell readers how X and Y are similar to or different from each other on that particular point. When giving details, you need to include the information from your research.

Below you can see an example of the first body paragraph from one student, who discussed differences between Osaka City and Yokohama City. Although this student did a nice job of doing research on the histories of the two cities, the references (the sources of information) are not provided here, because at this point the students had not yet learned how to cite sources in their papers (for more information, see Chapter 12).

> One important difference is their histories. By the 6th century, Osaka, which used to be called *Naniwa* at that time, developed into a hub port connecting the Kinki region to the western part of Japan and other countries, such as China and Korea. In 1496, a sect of *Jodo Shinshu* Buddhism established the *Ishiyama Hongan-ji* Temple, so that Osaka started to grow into a temple town. In the Edo period, it became the commercial and financial capital of Japan. Though Tokyo has replaced Osaka as the economic metropolis of Japan, Osaka is still the central city of West Japan. In contrast, the history of Yokohama is much shorter. Yokohama had been a fishing village until the middle of the 19th century. In 1859, because it was located near *Edo,* the former name of Tokyo, Yokohama Port was opened under the Treaty of Amity and Commerce with the United States and other countries. It became the base of foreign trade in Japan, so that many aspects of foreign cultures, such as newspapers, telegraphy, ice cream, and so on, were introduced to Yokohama first. In the 20th century, due to the growth of Japanese industry, it rapidly became a manufacturing city. In this way, the two cities have very different histories.

Although this is only the first paragraph of the body section, you can see how much detail the student put into this paragraph.

Conclusion
After you finish the three paragraphs of the body, there is only one paragraph left: the conclusion. Usually the conclusion and the introduction are connected; the concluding paragraph includes a restatement of the thesis statement in the introduction. After the restatement of the thesis statement, you should add a summary of the similarities or differences discussed in the body paragraphs. Moreover, in the end you can add your own perspective or informed opinion on the two subjects. Look at the sample concluding paragraph from the waltz and rumba paper introduced above (Introduction example 2).

> In conclusion, although the waltz and the rumba are both categorized as popular styles of ballroom dance, they have many significant differences in dancing posture, music and costume. Still there might be some people who claim that they are so ignorant about ballroom dance that they will not be able to distinguish a waltz from a rumba even after reading this explanation. Nevertheless, if they come to a ballroom dance competition once and see a real dance, they will soon find the clear differences in the points mentioned above and be able to understand ballroom dance better.

2. A final piece of advice

The purpose of showing these lessons on comparison/contrast was to give you an idea about how to get the structures right in the entire paper. Thus, I did not give you any examples of revising drafts or incorporating peers' or teacher's comments in your drafts (Chapter 14 deals with peer review). However, getting others' comments and revising your drafts are a very important part of writing an academic paper, as you already learned in Part II.

References

Folse, K., Muchmore-Vokoun, S., & Solomon, E. V. (2004). *Great essays: An introduction to writing essays* (2nd ed.). New York: Houghton Mifflin.

Huizenga, J., Snellings, C. M., & Francis, G. B. (1997). Comparison and contrast. In H. Yada, T. Kawahara, H. Kasuya, & Y. Sato (Eds. & Trans.), *Introduction to essay writing: A step-by-step course from paragraph to essay*. Tokyo: Shohakusha (pp. 76–95). (Original work published in 1990 by Heinle & Heinle).

Chapter 14

Peer Review: Editing an Academic Paper

These tasks have been used in academic writing classes at Kyoto University. Please try them.

1. Exploring preferences about correction and advice

Answer the questions below and compare your responses with those of classmates.

- a. Do you think that teachers should correct your writing mistakes?
- b. How have your English teachers helped you with writing problems?
- c. What did you like about the way those teachers helped you?
- d. What did you dislike about the way those teachers helped you?
- e. Do you think that suggestions by teachers help you improve your English? Explain.

2. Error correction

Learning Task 1

Correct the sentences below.

Original	Correction
1. He have been doing fieldwork for six months.	1.
2. It is a very impressed report.	2.
3. He told that the results were unclear.	3.
4. I respond to that survey last week.	4.
5+. Roots imbibe water nutrients from the soil. (add a word)	5+.
5-. Employees have no incentive that to work harder. (delete a word)	5-.
6. The sun emerged behind from the clouds.	6.
7. My paper was late. Because I couldn't print it.	7.
8. An accident occured.	8.
9. Where is your evidence.	9.
10. I am studying english.	10.
11. This data contains a error.	11.
12. He erased input for stimulate. [ignore this]	
13. Projections for public pensions in OECD countries show Japan's will be the second lowest, 22 percent of Japanese aged over 65 had incomes at 33.9% of salaries.	13.
14. The electrode is immersed on the solution.	14.

Learning Task 2

Check your corrections with those of a classmate. If you cannot agree on a correction, ask your teacher.

3. Local factor focus: using the writing correction guide

Learning Task 3

See the *Academic Writing Correction Guide* at the end of this chapter. Work with a partner to correct the following sentences. Try to discuss these problems using English as much as possible.

These examples are adapted from Kyoto University undergraduate student papers.

Example: This project have many researcher. [Error numbers:1, 2]
Revision: *This project has many researchers.*

A: I think one error is a number one, subject-verb agreement. Do you agree?
B: Yes, and another error is a number two, word form.
A: Where?
B: Researcher should be plural.

a. My acquaintance joins volunteer group in India now.
   [Error numbers:]
   Revision:

b. Her piano teacher was a very important influence to her.
   [Error numbers:]
   Revision:

c. A good way to learning a new language is by use Internet resources.
   [Error numbers:]
   Revision:

d. The grammar-translation method is more good way then communicative language learning.
   [Error numbers:]
   Revision:

e. MATSUKATA notes that: "By 1879 inflation had reached an alarming rate in Japan," due to the cost of the 1877 Satsuma Rebellion!
   [Error numbers:]
   Revision:

f. Firstly, some researchers argue if that the cloning techniques become common, humans might not set high values on animals.
   [Error numbers:]
   Revision:

g. I believe that humans should not attempt to clone mamoths since the result are too unpredictable.
   [Error numbers:]
   Revision:

h. Climate scientists around the world almost warn of the dangerous climate change.
   [Error numbers:]
   Revision:

i. The content of class of university are unique and interesting , But the some professor's skill of teaching are worse than high school teachers.
   [Error numbers:]
   Revision:

j. Globalization is very important in 21th century because the diversification of the nation leads more creativity and enhances the energy of society.
   [Error numbers:]
   Revision:

4. Global factor focus

4.1 Awareness of global errors

The *Academic Writing Correction Guide* focuses on local (or micro) errors, but you must also look for global (or macro) errors in your papers. Here are some of the common global problems in academic papers written by Kyoto University undergraduates.

a) Poor organization: e.g., weak introduction/conclusion, paragraphs/sections unclear/not logical, incorrect organization for the assignment
b) Formatting errors: e.g., paper not double spaced, paragraphs not indented, small font, no page numbers, incorrect margins, incorrect referencing
c) Content problems: e.g., weak thesis statement, confusing main points, not enough details (examples and explanation), lack of research/reading or poor sources
d) Writing style: e.g., weak topic sentences, lack of transitions within and between paragraphs/sections, too many simple sentences/words

4.2 Self-assessment

Learning Task 4

Based on your previous academic writing, which of these four areas do you believe to be areas of strength and weakness for you?

| I think that my essays generally have good (formatting, organization, content, writing) because _____ | My academic writing to date indicates that my (formatting, organization, content, writing) needs improvement. I think the area in which I need the most improvement is _____ because _____ |

4.3 Formulating and asking questions about your academic writing

It is important to share your work with others and to read the writing of your peers (classmates). This information exchange is essential because it gives you ideas about how to improve your writing. You need to practice reading your own writing and the writing of your peers critically. The beginning of critical reading involves finding problem areas in a paper.

Step 1: Finding problem areas

Learning Task 5

Read the following student paper* and underline the problem areas. After you finish, check your work with that of a classmate. (*This paper has been altered.)

Human Cloning

Introduction

The recent progress of genetic engineering is great. The first cloned animal, a sheep named Dolly, was born in 1997. Since then, the technology for cloning has advanced. In this essay, I will explain the advantages and disadvantages of cloning in these sections: domestic animals, medicines, endangered and extinct species, and cloning humans.

Before explaining good and bad points, I will explain cloning. Cloning is the process of making new organisms that have the same genes as the original organism. In artificial cloning, clones can be made in two ways...

Domestic Animals
People want to eat good quality food. Using cloning technology, we will be able to raise good quality beef cattle and cows in milk, because if we could meet the good quality cows, we could produce a lot of

the same genetic cows through cloning. This would give us endless supplies of beef and milk, but there are risks. A virus could mutate in the process of cloning (SHIMOMURA, 2002).

Medicines

When pharmacists make medicines, they often need proteins. But the structure of proteins is so complicated that it is difficult to makes a lot of proteins. Through cloning they will be able to make a lot of the same proteins. Therefore, they can make medicines more easy and efficient. Nevertheless, there can be safety problems due to cloning…

Extinct and Endangered Species

Cloning technology may save endangered species and might help the rebirth of extinct ones. For instance, there is a plan to reproduce the mammoth through the frozen cells. It could be possible in the future, however, when extinct species are cloned successfully, there are possibilities that they will not be able to adjust to Earth's current environment. Also, they could actually damage the ecosystem. Then, there is a possibility that not only revived animals, but also present animals will be extinguished.

Cloned human

The development of cloning technology means that we can make cloned organs and even, in theory, cloned humans. Cells from our own organs could be cloned to make replacement organs. There are many problems with this, however. First, …

Third, there are ethical issues involved. The cloned human has rights as a human, but cloned humans might not be treated as people. In other words, they might be treated more like machines or tools.

Conclusion

I think that cloning technology is excellent, but it is also terrible. We will be able to get a lot of benefits because of cloning technology. We will be faced with a lot of dangers we have never met, too. In my opinion, cloning technology will allow man to act like god and

> this is wrong. We should realize that life is important and precious. So, I think that advances of cloning technology should be kept to a minimum. We are only humans so we shouldn't violate the territory of god. Also, we must be very careful not to treat life as a mechanical process or humans as tools.

Step 2: Asking appropriate peer advice questions
Asking specific questions about your writing is an important skill to develop. Many students ask very broad, unspecified questions such as these:

- Can you fix my writing?
- Can you check my grammar?
- Can you tell me what is wrong with my paper?

Questions like these indicate that the student is not actively thinking about how to improve his/her writing. This is the lazy way to get help and is not appreciated. The more effective way to improve your academic writing is to be actively engaged in the writing process. Here are some examples of more specific questions practiced by some students at Kyoto University.

Learning Task 6

Look at the paper "Human Cloning" again and work with partners to think of possible peer advice. Write clear and specific questions for those problem areas without questions written.

1) People want to eat good quality food.
Problem: paragraph formatting (OK?)
Question: *Is my paragraph formatting okay?*
Advice: No, you need to indent the third paragraph.

2) In this essay, I will explain the advantages and disadvantages of cloning in these sections: domestic animals, medicines, endangered and extinct species, and cloning humans.
Problem: thesis statement (clear?)
Question: *Is my thesis statement clear?*
Advice:

3) Cloning is the process of making new organisms that have the same genes as the original organism. In artificial cloning, clones can be made in two ways ...
Problem: missing information (explain natural cloning?)
Question: *Do I need to explain what natural cloning is?*
Advice:

4) This would give us endless supplies of beef and milk, but there are risks. ∧A virus could mutate in the process of cloning (SHIMOMURA, 2002).
Problem: transitional phrase (need?)
Question: *Do I need a transitional phrase here (∧)?*
Advice:

5) A virus could mutate in the process of cloning (SHIMOMURA, 2002).
Problem: referencing style (correct?)
Question:
Advice:

6) A virus could mutate in the process of cloning (SHIMOMURA, 2002).∧
Problem: details (more?)
Question:
Advice:

7) Therefore, they can make medicines more easy and efficient.
Problem: grammar (OK?)
Question:
Advice:

8) Cloning technology may save endangered species and might help the rebirth of extinct ones ∧ .
Problem: information source (cite?)
Question:
Advice:

9) I think that cloning technology is excellent, but it is also terrible ∧ .
Problem: add word (technology?)
Question:
Advice:

10) We will be able to get a lot of benefits because of cloning technology. We will be faced with a lot of dangers we have never met, too.
Problem: combine sentences (how?)
Question:
Advice:

• Do you or your classmates see any other problems with this paper?

11) _____

Problem:
Question:
Advice:

12) _____

Problem:
Question:
Advice:

5. Global factor focus: getting peer advice

5.1 Asking specific peer advice questions

Here is a small sample of some possible questions you can ask classmates for advice.

Sample of Specific Peer Advice Questions

- Is there enough background information in my introduction?
- Can you understand this sentence?
- Can you think of a better word to use instead of _____?
- Is this section interesting?
- Is my page formatting correct?
- Do I need to explain/define this word?

Look at the questions in Step 2 above. Do you want to add some of them to those in the box?

More peer advice questions

5.2 Discuss and revise your academic paper

Learning Task 7

A. Read your paper and mark places (e.g., use numbers or ∧) where revisions are necessary.
B. On a different paper, write specific questions about the areas you marked.
C. Exchange papers with a classmate.
D. Read your classmate's paper silently and then offer him/her your advice.
E. Ask your peer advice questions. (**Revise your paper if you think it is necessary.**)
F. If you have time, read your paper aloud to your classmate. Does any part sound strange? Is anything difficult to understand? Listen carefully.

6. Academic writing correction guide

1	Subject-Verb Agreement	*He have been doing fieldwork for six months. He has been doing fieldwork for six months.
2	Word Form	*It is a very impressed report. It is a very impressive report.
3	Word Choice	*He told that the results were unclear. He said that the results were unclear.
4	Verb Tense	*I respond to that survey last week. I responded to that survey last week.
5	+ Add a Word	*Roots imbibe water nutrients from the soil. Roots imbibe water and nutrients from the soil.
	− Delete a Word	*Employees have no incentive that to work harder. Employees have no incentive to work harder.
6	Word Order	*The sun emerged behind from the clouds. The sun emerged from behind the clouds.
7	Sentence Fragment	*My paper was late. Because I couldn't print it. My paper was late because I couldn't print it.

8	Spelling	*An accident occured.* An accident occurred.
9	Punctuation	*Where is your evidence.* Where is your evidence?
10	Capitalization	*I am studying english.* I am studying English.
11	Article	*This data contains a error.* This data contains an error.
12	Meaning Not Clear	*He erased input for stimulate.* (Cannot understand the meaning.)
13	Run-on Sentence	*Projections for public pensions in OECD countries show Japan's will be the second lowest, 22 percent of Japanese aged over 65 have incomes at 33.9 percent of salaries.* Projections for public pensions in OECD countries show Japan's will be the second lowest as 22 percent of Japanese aged over 65 have incomes at 33.9 percent of salaries.
14	Preposition	*The electrode is immersed on the solution.* The electrode is immersed in the solution.

Chapter
15

Academic Writing in the Hybrid Classroom

This chapter introduces an academic writing course in the Liberal Arts and General Education curriculum at Kyoto University. The course is a semester-long elective among several other types of academic English courses for second-year undergraduates (e.g., academic reading, academic speaking, and academic listening). Each class session meets either once or twice per week for ninety minutes in a classroom equipped with a computer connected to the Internet for each student and the teacher. Students in the course major in a variety of subject areas such as agriculture, engineering, medicine, literature, economics, pharmacy, and law.

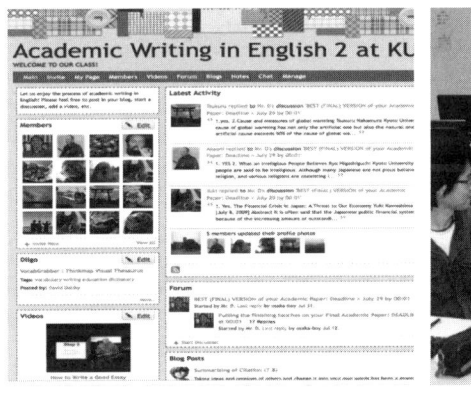

Figure 15.1 The hybrid classroom (digital/traditional)

1. Goals and expectations of the course

The concrete goal of the course is for students to complete a quality research paper written in English with at least 2,000 words plus references citations. By the end of the semester, students who actively participate should be able to do the following:

- Critically read academic texts about Japanese culture and society
- Provide critical feedback to peers
- Develop, organize, and support an academic argument with evidence from credible sources on a specific topic or issue related to Japanese culture or society
- Use in-text citations and reference citations correctly according to APA (American Psychological Association) style

Strict expectations are set for the course regarding punctuality, attendance, and homework. Students are expected to attend all of the classes, arrive at the classroom on time, actively participate in peer-to-peer activities and online discussions, and submit weekly homework assignments through the blog in the digital classroom. Homework assignments and in-class writing assignments (over 250 words per week) correspond to the research paper writing process as discussed in Part 2 of this book.

2. Description of the traditional classroom

The teacher's role in the traditional classroom is not a lecturer, but rather, a facilitator of critical reading, critical writing, and critical thinking. Lectures in the course take the form of brief writing tutorials. Before, after, or between these tutorials, discussion activities based on the students' homework assignments allow peer-to-peer learning to freely steer the class with the occasional guidance from the teacher. Students talk or write in English for the majority of the ninety minutes during the class sessions. Rotating the students' seating positions in the classroom every ten or fifteen minutes usually allows each student to exchange critical oral feedback with every student in the class and the teacher; indeed, through this activity, the class becomes an academic writing community.

2.1 Feedback

Both peer-to-peer and teacher-to-student feedback focuses on:
- paragraph structure;
- constructing, developing, and supporting an argument;
- synthesizing, evaluating, summarizing, paraphrasing, and quoting credible

academic sources of information, including correct use of in-text and reference citations;
- paper organization;
- attention to APA style; and
- frequently occurring sentence-level mistakes or repetitious patterns.

3. Description of the digital classroom

3.1 Ning: A Web-based social network platform

The digital component of this course is a Web-based social network platform called Ning (http://www.ning.com/). Anyone can create a private or public Ning social network for a fee. Ning can be used for private classrooms or for any type of interest group that can be open to the public. No special server, software, or equipment is required to use Ning; only a computer with a Web browser and an Internet connection. Furthermore, a Ning network is relatively easy to create and manage.

If you are interested in creating your own Ning network, try to do an Internet search with a key phrase such as "how to create your own social network on Ning" for instructions. Once a Ning network is created, the colors, designs, and fonts are customizable, or the network creator can choose from among 50 pre-set designs. Also, the network creator can freely choose a language for the Ning interface from among 25 options including Japanese. Students can sign up to join a Ning classroom network created by their teacher by accessing a webpage and entering only two pieces of required information: a name, which can be a screen name, and a computer email address.

3.2 Main page of a Ning

The features and their locations on the main page of a Ning are customizable. The following is a list of suggestions for how teachers can use these features in an academic writing class, but of course, teachers can freely use them in any way they choose:

- A place for each member's photo: Each student can choose to upload a photo or image.
- Blogging activity: Homework assignments can be submitted as blog posts.
- Discussion forum activity: In-class activities and homework assignments can be announced and discussed here.
- A chat room: A platform for the class to communicate online for questions, instructions, and discussions from either inside the walls of a traditional classroom or from a home, a library, a computer lab, a coffee shop, or a park bench—anywhere with Internet access.
- A box for notes: Lecture notes and useful websites can be placed here.
- RSS feeds: Information can be collected from social bookmarking sites such as Diigo (http://www.diigo.com/) for class activities aimed at researching

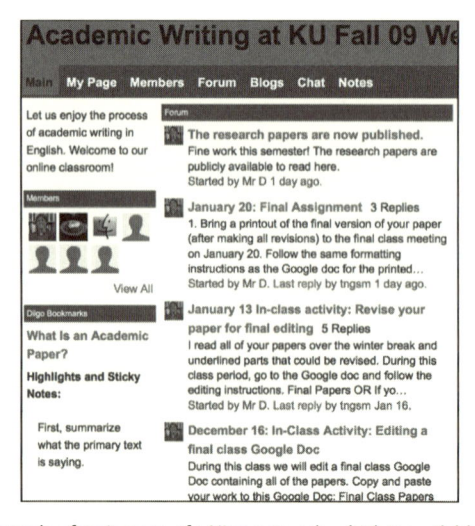

Figure 15.2 An example of main page of a Ning network, which is available for public viewing here: http://aw2atkufall09wed.ning.com/

and evaluating information from academic sources on the Web.
- Groups: Students can work in groups and communicate with their group members through a group network inside of the entire class network.
- Videos: Lectures about academic writing or academic content courses from universities can be uploaded from Academic Earth (http://www.academicearth.org/), for example.
- Other Ning features: Third-party applications, photos, events, music, a text box, a general activity box, and a box for a description of the social network are available.

3.3 Student page of a Ning

When Ning is used as a digital classroom, each student has his or her own page, which by default settings, is open to any member of the class to view including the teacher. Viewing a student's page makes it possible for the teacher to quickly assess the student's progress and activity in the course by looking at the number of blog posts and contributions to discussion forums at any time. Electronic files such as MS Word, MS PowerPoint, or PDF files can be attached to blog posts or discussion forum contributions.

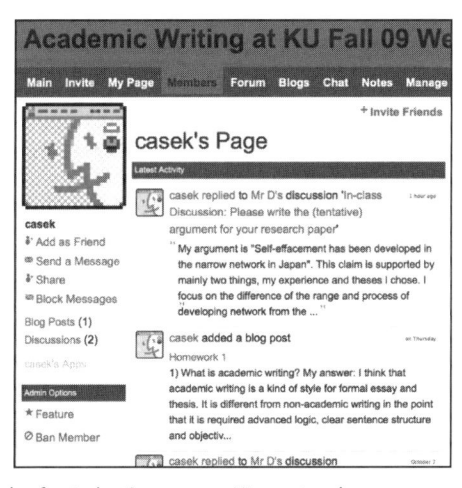

Figure 15.3 An example of a student's page on a Ning network

4. Features of the hybrid classroom

The hybrid classroom can offer the benefits of both traditional and digital classrooms. For example:
- Peer-to-peer and teacher-to-student interaction is possible outside of regularly scheduled class hours; the class could meet online in the case of a flu pandemic, for example.
- A chat room attracts students who may be overly concerned with face-maintenance; screen names create a sense of real or perceived anonymity.
- Students and the teacher can monitor and reflect on learning developments by reading a history of homework blog posts or discussion forum posts.
- During any class session, especially when students are refusing to speak face-to-face in English, the class can meet in the chat room to communicate through written English.
- Students can learn from each other by reading the work of peers and reading the feedback on the Ning, which can motivate students to try harder and learn from not only their own mistakes through self-revision activities and teacher feedback, but also from the mistakes of other students that are corrected by peers or by the teacher.
- A strict deadline can be set for homework assignments and the online platform all but eliminates excuses for students forgetting to bring their homework to class.
- Teachers can more easily manage collecting and reading weekly homework assignments with a paperless online social network such as Ning.

5. Independent learning in the global digital classroom

Before the Internet, academic information was scarce and shared by only an elite few. Now we live in a digital information age where even academic information is available to anyone with relatively unrestricted Internet access. The Internet provides endless opportunities for life-long independent learning. Students can visit the websites listed below, in addition to their brick-and-mortar university library, as places to start to find academic information in English and for advice with their academic writing. It is worth repeating here that *students should engage in their own independent critical evaluation of the source of any piece of information, especially sources found on the Internet* (see Chapter 7). Moreover, after their own independent evaluations, teachers may also find the following websites helpful for their classes, research, and professional development.

The following list introduces only a few of the many useful websites available on the Internet for English for Academic Purposes, especially those related to academic writing; teachers and students should search for more on their own to discover and share.

5.1 Credible sources of information on the Internet

- Peer-Reviewed Instructional Materials Online Database (PRIMO): http://www.ala.org/apps/primo/public/search.cfm
This is a database of peer-reviewed instructional materials about accessing, discovering, and evaluating information.

- The Internet Public Library (ipl2): http://www.ipl.org/
Here you can find annotated lists of websites organized by subject and free full-text sources of literature on the Web. The Internet Public Library is developed and maintained by library and information science professionals and students from a consortium of information science programs of universities and colleges from around the world, but mostly the USA.

- BUBL Catalogue of Internet Resources: http://bubl.ac.uk
A selection of academic resources for all subject areas, developed and maintained by the BUBL Information Service, Centre for Digital Library Research, Strathclyde University, Scotland.

5.2 Online textbooks and writing center homepages

- Using English for Academic Purposes: A Guide for Students in Higher Education: Academic Writing: http://www.uefap.com/writing/

- Dartmouth College Institute for Writing and Rhetoric Online Writing Materials: http://www.dartmouth.edu/~writing/materials/

- Purdue University Online Writing Lab (OWL): http://owl.english.purdue.edu/owl/

- University of Toronto Advice on Academic Writing: http://www.writing.utoronto.ca/advice

- Central European University Center for Academic Writing Self-access: http://web.ceu.hu/writing/sfaccess.html

5.3 Citations and APA style online tutorials

- Harvard University APA Exposed Online Tutorial: http://isites.harvard.edu/icb/icb.do?keyword=apa_exposed

- University of Auckland Referencite Interactive Tutorials: http://www.cite.auckland.ac.nz/index.php?p=tutorials

5.4 Technical and scientific writing

- Pennsylvania State College of Engineering: http://writing.engr.psu.edu/

- The Mayfield Handbook of Technical and Scientific Writing: http://www.mhhe.com/mayfieldpub/tsw/home.htm

5.5 More information

- RefSeek.com: http://www.refseek.com/directory/writing_grammar.html
  Here you can find links to a number of style guides besides the American Psychological Association (APA) guide. If you are writing in the humanities, for example, you might use the Modern Language Association (MLA) style or the Chicago Manual of Style. Also, check RefSeek.com for links to reference sources on the Web.

Index

A
abstract 60, 65, 113
academic audience 76
academic community 10, 48, 49
academic discourse community 77
Academic freedom 53
academic texts 11
academic vocabulary 11, 32, 37
Academic Word List 37
academic words 37
Academic Writing Correction Guide 189
American Psychological Association (APA) 164
argumentation 128, 143, 146
argumentation paper 144

B
body 135

C
cause and effect 115, 141, 145
citation 161
clarity 51
coherence 138
comparison and contrast 126, 142, 146
comparison/contrast 177
compound construction 24, 25
conclusion 61, 66, 151
Create-A-Research-Space (CARS) model 19, 21
credible sources 89
critical reading 53
critical thinking 47, 51–53, 62

D
digital information 206
discussion 66
diving 57, 62, 65, 66

E
EGAP vocabulary 37, 38
English for Academic Purposes (EAP) 13, 14
English for General Academic Purposes (EGAP) 13, 14
English for General Purposes (EGP) 13
English for Occupational Purposes (EOP) 13
English for Specific Academic Purposes (ESAP) 13, 14
English for Specific Purposes (ESP) 13
ESAP vocabulary 37, 38
evidence 144

F
full-sentence construction 24, 25

G
genre analysis 19, 20
genres 10, 20

H
headings 65
hedges 12
hybrid classroom 206
hypothesis 61

I
interrogative 25
in-text citations 162
introduction 11, 20–23, 60, 66, 123

J
jargon 32

K
keywords list 65

L
literature review 60, 114
long quotations 104

M

move 19–21
move analysis 21

N

Ning 203
nominal-group construction 24, 25
note taking 63

O

objectivity 12
originality 49
outline 75

P

paragraphs 136
paraphrasing 106
plagiarism 11, 12, 50
point-by-point method 180
primary sources of information 94
proceedings 48
process-oriented approach 25
productive vocabulary knowledge 35, 36
product-oriented approach 25

Q

quotations 102

R

receptive vocabulary knowledge 35
reference citation 163
references 50, 61, 66
register 32
research paper 10, 19
research questions 61, 76
rhetorical modes 82
rhetorical patterns 141

S

scanning 57, 63, 65
secondary sources 94
short quotations 102
skimming 57, 62, 66
skipping 57, 63, 66
step 20
steps 21
summarizing 109

T

technical words 26, 37
text coverage 33
thesis statement 79, 124, 129
title 23–26, 60, 65, 78, 79
Topic sentences 136
transitional words 145
transition words 138, 146

U

unity 137

V

vagueness 51
vocabulary 25
vocabulary knowledge 31–33, 41
vocabulary size 36, 37, 39

W

word family 33, 36
working thesis statement 81
working title 79
writing style 11

Kyoto University Academic Writing Research Group
（京都大学アカデミックライティング研究会）

The Kyoto University Academic Writing Research Group (KUAWRG) was founded in April 2007 by teachers in the Liberal Arts and General Education program and the Graduate School of Human and Environmental Studies. The KUAWRG was formed for the purpose of improving the English for General Academic Purposes (EGAP) program at Kyoto University by conducting research on EGAP writing course teaching/learning materials and methodology. The editors and authors are all members of this research group.

● Editorial Team （編集代表）

Akira Tajino, Tim Stewart, and David Dalsky

● Authors （著者）

Akira Tajino （田地野　彰）
Chapter 1, Chapter 2 (S. Maswana, C. Smith, and A. Tajino), and Chapter 3 (A. Tajino and T. Kanamaru)

Tim Stewart （ティム・スチュワート）
Chapter 6, Chapter 10 (T. Stewart and D. Dalsky), Chapter 11, Chapter 12 (D. Dalsky and T. Stewart), and Chapter 14

David Dalsky （デビッド・ダルスキー）
Chapter 7, Chapter 10 (T. Stewart and D. Dalsky), Chapter 12 (D. Dalsky and T. Stewart), and Chapter 15

Mayumi Fujioka （藤岡真由美）
Chapter 8, Chapter 9, and Chapter 13

Craig Smith （クレイグ・スミス）
Chapter 2 (S. Maswana, C. Smith, and A. Tajino), Chapter 4, and Chapter 5

Toshiyuki Kanamaru （金丸敏幸）
Chapter 3 (A.Tajino and T. Kanamaru) and Japanese Notes

Sayako Maswana （マスワナ紗矢子）
Chapter 2 (S. Maswana, C. Smith, and A. Tajino)

● Consultants （執筆協力）

Kohji Katsurayama （桂山康司）　　Nancy Lee （ナンシー・リー）
Sachi Takahashi （高橋　幸）　　　Hajime Terauchi （寺内　一）
Miki Hattori （服部美樹）　　　　　Yosuke Sasao （笹尾洋介）
Kazuya Yasuhara （安原和也）

Notes on the Contributors
（著者紹介）

AKIRA TAJINO, Ph.D., is Professor of Educational Linguistics at Kyoto University and coordinates the Kyoto University Academic Writing Research Group. His research interests include EAP, pedagogical grammar, and vocabulary learning and teaching. He is the author, or co-author, of several books, including *Tsukuru Eigo wo Tanoshimu* (Maruzen, 1999), *Korekara no Daigaku Eigo Kyoiku* (Iwanami Shoten, 2005), and *Researching Language Teaching and Learning: An Integration of Practice and Theory* (Peter Lang, 2009). He has published articles in a number of international journals, including *ELT Journal, Journal of English for Academic Purposes, Language, Culture and Curriculum,* and *Language Teaching Research.*

TIM STEWART teaches academic writing at Kyoto University. He has published numerous articles and book chapters in academia. He is the former editor of the international TESOL association journal *Essential Teacher* and currently edits the Communities of Participation section of the *TESOL Journal.*

DAVID DALSKY is an associate professor at Kyoto University. He holds a Ph.D. in social psychology and his research interests in that field include social cognition, self-esteem, and intercultural training. He has published papers in the *Journal of Cross-Cultural Psychology, Asian Journal of Social Psychology, Journal of Personality and Individual Differences, Journal of Research in Personality,* and the *Encyclopedia of Applied Psychology.* He enjoys teaching undergraduate academic writing courses in hybrid classrooms using web-based tools and applications.

MAYUMI FUJIOKA is Associate Professor of English at Kinki University and also teaches academic writing courses at Kyoto University. She received her Ph.D. from Indiana University, U.S.A. Her research interests include second-language academic literacy development and interlanguage pragmatics. She has contributed chapters to several books, including *Learning the Literacy Practices of Graduate School* (University of Michigan Press) and *Pragmatics in Language Learning: Theory and Practice* (Japan Association for Language Teaching). She has also presented numerous papers in international conferences, including the *Symposium on Second Language Writing, AILA,* and *TESOL.*

CRAIG SMITH is Professor of English and Chair of the Department of Global Affairs at Kyoto University of Foreign Studies. He teaches an academic writing course and an academic oral presentation course at Kyoto University. He has many experiences in presenting papers at international conferences, including IATEFL, KATE, and the Oxford University Conference on English Education in Kobe. He has published papers in books and international journals, including *Researching Language Teaching and Learning: An Integration of Practice and Theory* (Peter Lang, Switzerland) and *Language Teaching Research.*

TOSHIYUKI KANAMARU is an assistant professor in the Department of Foreign Language Acquisition and Education at Kyoto University. He holds a B.Sc. in Integrated Human Studies and a Ph.D. in Human and Environmental Studies, both from Kyoto University. His research interests include cognitive linguistics, natural language processing, vocabulary acquisition, and language education. He is a co-author of *Kyodai Gakujutsu Deitabeisu Kihon Eitango 1110.* [the Kyoto University Data-based List of 1,110 Essential Academic Words] (Kenkyusha, 2009).

SAYAKO MASWANA is an assistant professor in the Open Education Center at Waseda University. She is currently conducting research on genre analysis of research articles and academic writing. She has published in a number of journals such as *Kyoto University Researches in Higher Education* and *Classroom Research at the International Exchange Center, Nara Women's University.* She is a co-author of *Kyodai Gakujutsu Deitabeisu Kihon Eitango 1110.* [the Kyoto University Data-based List of 1,110 Essential Academic Words] (Kenkyusha, 2009).

Writing for Academic Purposes 英作文を卒業して英語論文を書く

発行	2010年4月6日　初版1刷
	2015年3月16日　4刷
定価	2000円＋税
編者	田地野 彰、ティム・スチュワート、デビッド・ダルスキー
発行者	松本 功
装幀組版	大崎善治
印刷製本所	株式会社 シナノ
発行所	株式会社 ひつじ書房
	〒112-0011 東京都文京区千石2-1-2 大和ビル2F
	Tel.03-5319-4916　Fax.03-5319-4917
	郵便振替 00120-8-142852
	toiawase@hituzi.co.jp　http://www.hituzi.co.jp/

ISBN978-4-89476-490-3

造本には充分注意しておりますが、落丁・乱丁などがございましたら、小社かお買上げ書店にておとりかえいたします。ご意見、ご感想など、小社までお寄せ下されば幸いです。